T0339665

"This book is a transformative read that speaks directly to the essence of true leadership and personal development. Through a blend of unique insights and practical advice, Payal demystifies the journey to professional excellence, making it accessible to all. This book is a testament to her profound understanding of leadership dynamics and her ability to articulate a path that bridges the gap between potential and achievement. It's a must-read for anyone aiming to unlock their true leadership powers and ascend to new heights in their career. Highly recommended."

Nick Jonsson, Managing Director EGN
Singapore, Indonesia & Malaysia

"Payal, due to her close proximity to various great leaders has provided very good thought-provoking ideas and framework in finding interaction between inner and external powers. This book provides much-needed compelling ideas on the power of transforming ourselves to achieve our leadership potential and fulfillment in life by taking risks and charting unknown territories in complex ever-changing business environments."

Shailendra Jagtap, Managing Director & Country
Manager at John Deere India Pvt Ltd

"This book is a great resource for anyone who aspires to the top and is willing to give what it takes. This book describes what matters beyond hard work, dedication, and being at the right place at the right time very well."

Girisan Kariangal, Managing Director,
A. Menarini India Private Limited

"This book is a must-read if you want to break out from the self-imposed bonds holding you back. She is the best executive coach you could have drawing on the experience of the best leaders. I agree with her, the starting point is understanding yourself and what's holding you back. Then think strategically and use your self-confidence to take risks."

Frank O'Connell, Author of *Jump First Think Fast*

"Payal Nanjiani is great at bringing out the subtle yet powerful points that move the needle. In this book the weaving of the professional powers, inner leadership powers and outer leadership powers is beautiful. Combining this with the 'I need to take charge as the change needed is inside me…80% of the work is done inside the mind' concept is simply powerful. The other part about leaders being mind readers, and then the one about taking risks, is all invaluable and key to developing strong leadership and driving success."

Vishal Sharma, CEO, Godrej Industries Ltd

"Success in leadership roles requires the cultivation of many skills. The foremost of them is learning to lead yourself before you lead others. Payal Nanjiani, an expert leadership coach, has diligently deep-dived into the why and how of this. Her latest book inspires everybody on how to arrest self-made excuses for our mediocre behaviours, grow over our mental comforts, unlock our fears, and dismantle harmful habits and beliefs to conquer ourselves, for that is the way to the true north. Success is an internal game for which she has provided apt guidance on harnessing our ultimate potential and triumph in our careers."

Swami Mukundananda, Global Spiritual Leader and Mind Management Expert

"Payal has a rare ability to connect dots across the hundreds of deep conversations that she has with a broad spectrum of leaders, to create fresh insights on self, teams, and organizations."

Dr. Varun Nagaraj, Dean, SPJIMR, India

"Payal is fiercely optimistic. She looks for and finds that opportunity in every adversity with a calm, unruffled mind and smiling face. I have noticed her colleagues getting inspired by her innate problem-solving skills without being overbearing."

Dr. Arun Arora, Chairman, Vivero Preschools & Childcare

"This easy-to-read book takes one on a very interesting path of self-discovery in one's career field. The author with a very gentle nudge guides the understanding of the elements of not only individual leadership but the techniques as well."

Indrani Malkani, Ashoka Fellow, Chairman at
V Citizens Action Network (VCAN)

"Reading through this book I can proudly say this Wonder Woman has hit the bull's eye again. As both of us have brainstormed, the challenge most leaders face is their inability to realise not only their inherent potential but their team's as well to move from good to great. This book will help unravel this mystery especially as Payal dwells on the concept of 'inner leadership' and 'outer leadership' and finding the right balance between the two and unleashing one's full leadership potential! Kudos to her not only elevating her game but helping others elevate their game as well."

D. Narain, Partner AgVaya and retired President & CEO of
Bayer South Asia and Global Head of Smallholder Farming

Make It To the Top

You are working hard. You are sustaining your job. You are doing well in your field. Life seems fine. But there is something that's holding you back from making it to the top in your field of work. That something could be an annoying habit, a behavior, or a trait that's getting you stuck in your career.

All of us want promotions and salary increases. We desire to make it to the top. But most of us don't realize that these things cannot be asked for by putting our hands out.

You can get that promotion, the salary raise, the new project, the visibility, the sponsors, the accolades, and the achievements only when you work on yourself harder than you work on your job. You must become such that success, promotion, and job offers begin to follow you everywhere.

In this book, Payal Nanjiani points out that the reason why many do not make it to the top is not because of a lack of information, abilities, or skills. Having private access to some of the world's most successful industry leaders, she tells you that those who truly make it to the top in their careers are doing things differently than others.

An expert coach and business consultant who helps leaders globally overcome their unconscious habits and behaviors to attain higher levels of success, she has worked with corporates and leaders around the globe bringing about a huge transformation in the thinking and behaviors of leaders. Her one-on-one coaching comes with a six-figure price tag. But in this book, Payal shares some great advice and strategic solutions to reach the top without a hefty price tag.

The book has hands-on advice on what to do, how to do it, and what transformation to bring about in your thinking and habits. These ideas, powers, and habits have been tested in practice on numerous executives Payal has coached in the past eighteen years and are helpful to people in every part of the organization.

We all face challenges and deal with setbacks. But in the long run, you'll achieve incredible growth and success if you're willing to change your thinking and behaviors.

Are you ready to unlock your leadership powers and live your best life?

Make It To the Top

How to Use Your Traits,
Experiences, and Behaviors to
Achieve Limitless Growth for
Yourself and Your Organization

Payal Nanjiani

Routledge
Taylor & Francis Group

A PRODUCTIVITY PRESS BOOK

First published 2025
by Routledge
605 Third Avenue, New York, NY 10158

and by Routledge
4 Park Square, Milton Park, Abingdon, Oxon, OX14 4RN

Routledge is an imprint of the Taylor & Francis Group, an informa business

ISBN: 978-103-2-57384-7 (hbk)
ISBN: 978-103-2-57383-0 (pbk)
ISBN: 978-100-3-43913-4 (ebk)

DOI: 10.4324/9781003439134

Typeset in Minion
by Deanta Global Publishing Services, Chennai, India

To my awesome and enterprising daughter, to my best friend ever, Rishona Nanjiani on your 16th birthday.

You are God's blessing to me, and with you, life is at its best.

Contents

Foreword xiii

A Confession and a Promise from the Author xiv

Aligning the Two Leadership Powers... xxii

Acknowledgments xxv

About the Author...xxvi

PART 1   How to Become the Leader You Want to Be

Chapter 1 Define Your Top 3

Chapter 2 Sustain at the Top... 8

Chapter 3 The Future Is of a Meta-Leader.............................. 13

Chapter 4 Unleash the Meta-Leader from Within 18

Chapter 5 It Takes More Than Performance 21

PART 2   Using Your Leadership Powers

Power 1 Great Leaders Are Mind Readers................................. 27

Power 2 Radiate Positive Relational Energy 34

Power 3 Focus on Your Game.. 39

Power 4 Develop the Ability of Distanced Thinking.............. 45

Power 5 Work Like an Immigrant... 50

Power 6 Be Unpredictable 55

Power 7 Bet on Yourself 62

Power 8 Attract Your Sponsors... 70

Power 9 Sow and Reap Continuously....................................... 77

Power 10   Play Big.. 83

Power 11   The Devil Is in the Feedback........................... 88

Power 12   Train Your Brain to Say No 92

Power 13   Go for the Impossible...................................... 97

Power 14   Avoid Shiny Object Syndrome 102

Power 15   Use Your Million-Dollar Asset...................... 107

Power 16   Build Your Brand 112

Power 17   Make Speed Your Best Friend 118

Power 18   Optimize Your Weekends............................... 123

Power 19   Take Your People with You............................ 128

Power 20   Play Politics, but Come Out Clean............... 132

Power 21   Cut the Cord at the Right Time 137

Power 22   Build Emotion Strength................................. 142

PART 3   It's Not Lonely at the Top: It's Lonely All the Way to the Top

It's Not Lonely at the Top, It's Lonely All the Way........................... 151

Index... 159

Foreword

It is a great pleasure and honor to write a foreword for a talented author, expert coach, transformational leadership speaker, and a dear friend of mine Payal Nanjiani's latest work on leadership. In this insightful book, she delves into the intricacies of what it takes to *Make It To the Top* by drawing from both personal experiences and extensive research on leadership.

I've had the privilege of witnessing Payal's dedication for work and attention to detail during her course of assignment with us. Every aspect of her work reflects meticulous care, genuine concern, and hard work put in while working on her assignment.

When I look back on my learnings and experience working with global organizations, I strongly believe in building consensus with my team, listening to peers and stakeholders, empowering my team to execute and deliver the results. Also, an important part of my working style is through the PDCA cycle and firm execution of my decisions, which has always been my core strength.

In this ever-evolving landscape of leadership, navigating the complexities of guiding individuals and teams towards a common vision requires a lot of resilience and inner strength.

Throughout the pages, Payal offers valuable insights, practical strategies, and thought-provoking anecdotes that will challenge your perceptions and transform your approach to leadership. It will enable you to overcome your unconscious habits and behaviors to attain higher levels of success. Please note that it is not easy to be alone at the top.

I am confident that Payal's wisdom and expertise will leave an indelible mark on your leadership philosophy and equip you with the tools to lead with purpose, passion, and integrity.

With best wishes

Sandeep Singh
Managing Director
Tata Hitachi

A Confession and a Promise from the Author

I have a confession to make.

Though my books have been awarded the Books of Excellence, and The Times Group recognized me as the most influential leadership speaker and executive coach, life wasn't always like this for a girl born in India with an adult life in America.

Let me tell you something about my life and the transformation I had to bring to myself to have gotten where I am.

"How on the earth did I get here?" is a question people have asked me numerous times. But for the first time, I asked this question myself as I walked up the stage, clad in my blue shirt and black suit, to receive the prestigious Times Group Award for the most influential executive coach.

While walking up to the stage, I heard the presenter read my bio, saying that I was the only woman of color from India to be recognized as a leadership author and coach in a completely white male-dominated industry in America.

It was then when, for the very first time, I thought to myself that there were no authors or coaches in my family background. Then how did a woman of color like me, from a working-class family, compete and make a name in a predominantly white male-dominated society?

If you had met with me in 1996, when I completed my undergrad in economics, my life would have looked entirely different.

I was raised in a generation where girls were taught the art of taking care. My mom constantly reminded me to care of what I wear, how I walk and talk, and how to care for the house. Education and career were important, but society did not consider a career a big part of a woman's life.

After completing my undergrad in 1996, I had no clear goal or dream for my future. My mom thought it would be better if I got married as she kept speaking to me about it, and I would hear her out.

My father had a different opinion from everyone else around me. He encouraged me to study further and complete my Master's. I agreed, not because I liked the M.B.A., but because I got seduced by the societal norms of having an M.B.A. degree under your belt. And also because it would keep marriage off the chart for me for some time at least.

After completing my M.B.A., I started working. It is here that I dreamt of doing something big in my life. I imagined a life entirely of success. When I would tell my mom of my dreams, she would smile and calmly remind me that doing big things is not for everybody. She would often say that not everyone can be an Ambani or a Sam Walton, for that matter, and that they were born with something different in them, and everyone is not cut to make it to the top.

Her words made me feel I did not have that *"something"* in me to reach the top. And she was right. Even the business world would often portray successful people in ways that made all of us believe that they just had something in them that you and I did not.

My life dragged between office and home for the next seven years. I often would blame my luck, destiny, people, environment, boss, country, and everything around me for failure. I would also blame God for not giving me that "something" special in me to be successful.

Come 2001, I was an ordinary girl doing a nine-to-five job, working hard, and living the "American dream" to some extent. In the evening, I would meet up with friends or colleagues over a drink or dinner, and on weekends, I would relax, get a few D.V.D.s from Blockbuster (yeah, they existed at one time), or snuggle tight in bed for long hours.

I had yet to decide what to do with my personal and career life. I had a job, but I needed direction and a purpose. My self-worth was non-existent. I just felt like I was nowhere. I wasn't growing at work and had many failures at my jobs.

Growth, leadership roles, achieving something big in my career life, and making it to the top were not on my watch in those days.

Every time I hit rock bottom in my career, I would work on skilling and upskilling myself, listening to motivational tapes, and reading as much as possible to help improve my results in life. But I was in the same old cycle of procrastinating, binge-watching, and getting stuck in my career.

Yes, that was my life. Unbelievable as it may sound, it's the holy truth.

So, what changed, and how did I become one of the most well-known executive coaches? How did I become the first choice for Fortune 100 companies as a coach for their C.E.O.s and senior leadership teams? How did I reach the top in my field and be among the highest-paid executive coaches?

I have a lot to thank the universe and my father for this.

During those confusing and humdrum years of my career, my father put the seed of a dream into me, saying I could be anything I wanted to be and that life had many possibilities.

It was the first time someone had said something like this to me. Now, like me, if you've been in America for most of your life, then you know the market is flooded with self-development gurus and tapes that tell you to believe in yourself and that you can do just about anything.

But when the real people in your closest circle tell you the same things, it enters right into your soul.

I was hungry to make something out of myself (and frankly more terrified that I'd amount to nothing). I wanted to leave my mark on the world. I wanted to create history, not become history.

And so I began looking up books and the internet to know what it takes to reach the top.

And I found that the business world, like my wonderful mom, teaches us that not everyone can reach the top.

On the other hand, in the same business world, we are trained to maximize our potential, saying that we all can succeed and reach the top. Now, aren't these confusing messages?

Add to this the fact that our world is full of information on what it takes to succeed and reach the top.

The question that perturbed me was this: If everyone knows what it takes to be successful and all of us in the corporate world are "well-trained," then why are so many people in the workforce struggling to achieve their definition of success?

Why do so many people retire with a feeling of unfulfillment? Why do so many people's dreams die? Why can only a few of us make it to the top? Why?

By the time this book lands in your hands, I will have coached more than a thousand leaders and impacted the lives of more than a million professionals, helping them reach the top. As an executive coach, I know why many people don't get to the top.

Let me be honest here. The reason why many do not make it to the top is not because of a lack of information or skills. I have private access to some of the world's most successful industry leaders and can tell you that those who truly make it to the top in their careers are the ones who have followed a simple equation in their lives. That equation is as follows:

Making it to the top = 20% skills + 80% the person behind the skills (YOU)
(Figure 0.1)

The above equation tells us that to make it to the top, you must be willing to work more on yourself than on your job. It means that your skills need to be sharpened to help you keep up with the changes in your industry. However, the person behind the skills, you, plays a significant role.

Look at the figure. What we usually see in successful people is their 20%, which is their talent, skills, success, abilities, hardwork, money, position, titles, and accolades. What the business world does not show us is the actual 80%. This includes thinking, emotions, behaviors, habits, mastery, relentless, unstoppable, mental toughness, sacrifice, failures, persistence, innovation, vision, self-doubt, loneliness, passion, and dreams.

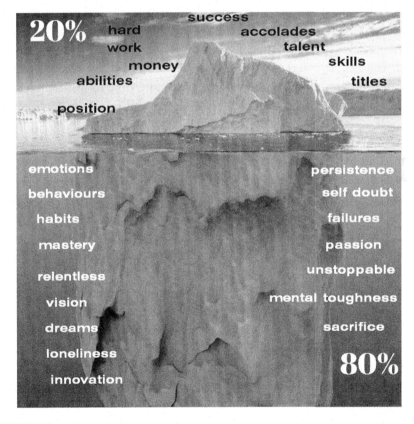

FIGURE 0.1
Iceberg.

Those who work hard on themselves instead of their job are invested in their personal development. They give time to themselves. Giving time to yourself for your internal development is the most expensive gift you can give yourself.

They are committed to bringing about a transformation in the way they think and behave.

Personally, I regret not knowing about this equation early on in my career.

My father once gave me advice, which helped me tremendously. He said, "Payal, nobody can give you wiser advice than yourself. So, at all times, keep uplifting yourself so that you give great advice to yourself."

He couldn't have been more right. Out of everyone you know, you are the only person always present in your life, nonnegotiable, day and night. And so it's essential that you consistently work on the most critical person in the world: yourself. When we have a harmonic relationship with ourselves, we no longer look to other people to fill the gaps in our self-esteem. We need people, but we aren't emotionally greedy or dependent. As Wayne Dyer said, "You can never feel lonely when you like the person you're alone with."

In our day-to-day corporate life, we need more time to work on developing ourselves. I encourage you to work on and invest in developing yourself.

The more you work on yourself, the sooner you will become aware of your leadership powers and how to leverage them. It means you become what I call a "meta-leader."

When you take the meta-leader approach, your career life will change.

One of the most significant challenges I have seen leaders face is identifying and using their leadership powers at work, and I've helped them overcome this challenge. It's all about understanding your leadership powers.

Knowing about my leadership powers and how I could leverage them was a defining moment in my career life.

Looking back on those years, I accomplished something rare when I began maximizing and fulfilling my potential. And the concepts in this book can help you fulfill your potential. It will get you to the top.

My life is not perfect. Things have happened and will continue to happen.

However, I am not so much concerned about what will happen because I have learned to unleash my leadership powers and have faith in a higher power.

A promise:

> To anyone who needs to hear this today, *There is no one, absolutely no one, whom the Universe has created to be unsuccessful. Each of us is here to succeed. We are here in the corporate world to make it to the top.*

As a child, I never actually believed much in myself. Like anyone else, I would often go with what others thought about me.

And as I stepped into the workforce, my focus was more on how to fit into a white male-dominated work culture in corporate America.

I never thought I would grow up to impact millions of lives globally. And that I would write award-winning books, coach high-end executives, and speak on stages globally.

But it happened to me. And it happened because I learned that one must never try to fit in when the universe has created you to be unique and stand out in ways only you can.

I hope this can be a testament and a reminder to YOU that you can achieve your dreams and do what you are created for.

Let's give more power to ourselves than to our environment. The most challenging part of leadership is accepting and utilizing your powers to achieve infinite possibilities for ourselves, the team, and the organization.

Every leader has powers, which I call "leadership powers." We all have them in abundance. You have two major professional powers: inner leadership powers and outer leadership powers. These powers, when used correctly, transform you to become a meta-leader. In the chapters ahead, you will read about your professional powers and the meta-leader.

To experience outer leadership powers, you must first develop your inner leadership powers. Both are tightly interconnected. An alignment of these two powers will help you reach the top.

You will read more about these powers and how to apply them daily. As you consistently increase the inherent power inside you, you'll begin to see an alternate reality flush with attractive opportunities and luxurious possibilities. Leadership is an inside game.

And I promise you, the more you believe in and apply these leadership powers, the more you will achieve your heart's content.

Many of us are afraid to step into our success because we are too busy comparing ourselves to someone else. You are unique and can make a difference.

As we move to the following few pages in the book, I will share with you the true, deep meaning of a meta-leader and how you can be one.

I don't promise this book will solve all your work-related problems. But I do promise from the depth of my heart that if you apply the lessons in this book, learn from the stories, take time to reflect on the powers, work on unleashing them, and take the leadership challenge at the end of each chapter, you will begin to see the difference in the quality of your work and results.

All of us want promotions and salary increases. We desire to make it to the top. But most of us don't realize that these things cannot be asked for by putting our hands out. You get that promotion, the salary raise, the new project, the visibility, the sponsors, the accolades, the achievements when you work on yourselves. It's time you become such that success, promotion, and job offers begin to follow you everywhere.

In these pages, you will learn how to be a meta-leader, a person of excellence, and with limitless growth. The powers mentioned in this book will open up the neural pathways of your brain and will prevent you from getting stuck in your career life.

The book has hands-on advice on what to do, how to do it, and what transformation to bring about in your thinking and habits. These ideas, powers, and habits have been tested in practice on numerous executives I have coached in the past fifteen years and are helpful to people in every part of the organization.

We all face challenges and deal with setbacks. But in the long run, you'll achieve incredible growth and success if you're willing to change your thinking and behaviors.

I promise this book will speed up your growth and success by giving you valuable techniques to become the best version of yourself.

Remember, success, growth, promotion, and visibility don't happen purely because of hardwork and effort; they occur as a result of the way you transform yourself in your habits.

The corporate world recently went through the impacts of the COVID-19 pandemic, followed by great resignation, and now the trend is about quitting quietly, with inflation and recession raising its head.

And so, fatigue and stress are plaguing organizations. Even the most resilient of business leaders still report being in survival mode.

When you awaken your inner and outer leadership powers, you discover your infinite potential to lead the self, the people, and the organization.

Derived from quantum physics, neuroscience, and the psychology of successful leaders, I have written this book for the millions of professionals who want to get to the next level, lead a life of significance, and create an impact in their field of work.

By the time you read this book, I would've helped millions of professionals around the globe to recognize their powers and achieve infinite possibilities. Many of today's C.E.O.s and government leaders I've coached are testimonials to the inner and outer leadership powers.

One thing I know for sure: by practicing all of these powers, by writing about them, and by living them every day, I have been transformed into a new person, a happier, more purposeful, more fully alive person than I ever dreamed possible for myself. Now, I hope that my efforts and energy are visible in this book and will help you make a positive, loving difference in your life.

I believe you have what it takes to make it in today's competitive and changing business environment.

I promise you that you can achieve everything you've wanted in your career if you are prepared to transform yourself.

Are you ready to unlock your leadership powers and live your best life?

God Bless.
Your Good Friend and Coach

Payal Nanjiani
2024

Aligning the Two Leadership Powers

I want to begin by asking you to tell yourself the below phrase with full conviction:

"Today onward, I am an unstoppable leader."

I asked you to do this not to just motivate you or create an aha moment. I asked you to do this because eighteen years back, when I left corporate America to do what I am now doing, the more I began associating and coaching with some of the top leaders in the corporate world, the more I understood that the actual game of success is completely internal.

And so, how far you will reach in your career, how much you will accomplish is dependent not just on your skills, abilities, or credentials. Predominantly it is dependent on the alignment of your professional powers; inner leadership powers, and outer leadership powers.

Today's leaders require to use their inner and outer professional powers to manage in an ever-changing, economically and culturally diverse, and constantly challenging environment.

The inner and outer leadership powers are in close interdependency, and thus any attempt to improve the perceivable leadership skills needs to start at the innermost layers.

However, some fail to understand the interdependency between the inner and outer leadership powers and thus adopt a shallow, ineffective approach.

Leaders need to maximize their inner and outer leadership powers to improve the way they lead.

THE INTERCONNECTION BETWEEN YOUR INNER AND OUTER LEADERSHIP POWERS

Each of us embodies the outer power and the inner power. Inner leadership powers bring together your behavior, thinking, mind, body, and soul.

It's the quiet force within you that knows when to act and when to move and gives you the strength to do so.

Few of us will ever harness our inner leadership powers to the fullest. Because of this, we often play average in our career life, just going from one position to another, one job to another, and one title to another.

We could actually accomplish so much more if we learned which inner leadership powers we must use.

When we don't develop and harness our inner leadership powers, we become accustomed to doing things the same way, thinking familiar thoughts, and following comfortable behavior patterns so that we don't have to invest too much energy in getting things done.

When you correctly leverage your inner leadership powers, it can give you miraculous results. This power is something we all have, but we need to learn how to tap into it in creative and effective ways in our daily life.

For example, the way you think has a significant impact on your career. Great leaders know that 80% of their work is done inside the mind. You *can* make a massive difference in your career, relationships, and total well-being by training your mind to succeed.

Outer leadership powers are about your position, talent, skills, results, and abilities. Your external leadership powers are as important as your inner leadership powers.

But many of us shy away from fully using our external leadership powers at work. They reject their external powers, labeling it a manipulative and dirty concept. Yet, without fully utilizing it, they are far more limited in the good they can bring to their organizations and the world.

True power is a combination of both internal and external power. When you don't want to be associated with using your professional powers, it leads to powerlessness. The truth is that power is not bad in and of itself; it is what you do with power that determines its ethics.

Great things happen when the inner and outer leadership powers are aligned. Our life experience unfolds in pleasantly inspired, easeful, and empowering ways.

On the other hand, when the inner and outer leadership powers are out of alignment, we tend to feel "off" in ways that sometimes we can't quite define. Stress, burnout, tension, self-doubt, lack of growth, and anxiety come in our way of success.

And, let's be honest here. In the corporate world, training is over-rated, and transformation is underrated. We believe the more training we receive, the better our chances of reaching the top.

In reality, because I have access to these successful leaders at the top, I can almost assure you that they are more about transformation than training. They focus well on aligning the two leadership powers, contributing to 80% of their success, and only 20% happens because of your functional and technical skill sets.

However, the majority of the workforce population does not focus on this 80%.

This book is about helping you discover and harness both of your leadership powers to reach the top.

Each one of us is great in our own way. Each one of us has exquisite powers within us. When you align your external leadership powers with your inner leadership powers, you will always have a competitive advantage over others in your field.

Your journey to the top will speed up threefold because now you will be able to overcome obstacles faster and lead through any challenges.

The best among us are not more gifted than the rest. They just make use of their powers each day as they march toward their biggest life. And days become months and months become years and before they know it, they have reached the top in their field of work.

I encourage you to not only read through this book, but to actually practice the leadership powers everyday and begin to see the growth in your career life.

Acknowledgments

This book would not have been possible without the contribution of many individuals.

I thank the editor and publisher, Routledge Publishers, for their continuous faith in me and my work.

Thank you to my wonderful team members, Jane M, Robert R, Lakshmi Chonat, Ishika Latwal and Meenakshi Satpathy for their continuous support and dedication. You all are the pillars of my work.

I appreciate the continuous support I get from my family, my dear husband Ashish, my wonderful daughters Ronisha and Rishona who push me out of my comfort zone, my loving parents Ashok and Laltoo Malkani for their unconditional love to me and my incredibley young at heart aunt Meenu who shows me what it is never give up on work.

To all my clients who have always trusted my work and who are unbelievably successful, yet strive to be better each day.

To my all-time mentor and friend Arun Arora, Chairman, Edvance & Former President Bennet Coleman & Company Ltd.

To the numerous management school faculty and students whom I teach my leadership principles.

About the Author

Recognized by the Times Group, Payal Nanjiani is an Indian-American globally acclaimed leadership expert, executive coach, and author.

As an executive coach, and buisness consultant Payal Nanjiani has advised and coached leaders of Fortune 500 companies, C.E.O.s, top executives, and government officials. She is one of the world's most accomplished and in-demand executive coaches.

A prominent figure in the corporate world, her training and coaching have brought about a transformation in the thinking and behavior of more than a million professionals globally.

She has spent over two decades advising organizations and their leaders on how to be peak performers, reach their next level, and achieve extraordinary success for themselves and the organization.

Payal has been a highly sought-after leadership speaker for organizations and conferences that have chosen Payal for their most important events. Her talks and training help people achieve a leadership breakthrough like never before.

In 2019 she launched *The Payal Nanjiani Leadership Podcast* to help people believe in their innate quality to lead and succeed. The podcast, which has been rated in the top 10% globally, features some of the most prominent leaders, spiritual gurus, and C.E.O.s in the world.

A New York award-winning author, Payal's books help you be a peak performer and reach your next level.

Payal has been honored and featured extensively on America's Fox 50 news channel, *Mumbai Mirror, Times of India* news, global magazines, and multiple worldwide media for her work in leadership.

Payal lives with her philosophy, "Leadership starts and ends with YOU,"™ and believes that you can achieve success in any economy.

She travels between her home in the United States and India.

Official Website: www.payalnanjiani.com

Reach out at payal@payalnanjiani.com

Awards and Accolades:

- Honored and featured in the US Media for redefining leadership and for being the only woman of Indian descent to be a recognized and powerful executive coach and author in America.
- Recognized by the Times Group as the Most Influential Personality in Leadership Speaking and Coaching.
- Recognized as the Top 10 Coach by Silicon India Magazine.
- Recipient of the State Ribbon award, USA, for her work in leadership.
- Recipient of the New York Book Award, USA, and Book of Excellence, Canada, for her books.
- Award-winning host of the globally recognized leadership mastery podcast *The Payal Nanjiani Leadership Podcast*.
- Recipient of the Prof. Indira J. Parikh International Award for global leadership coaching.
- Awarded the best Executive Coach 2024 by The World HRD Congress.

More books by Payal Nanjiani:

1. *Success Is Within: The 21 Ways for Achieving Results, Prosperity, and Fulfillment by Changing Your Leadership Mindset*
2. *Achieve Unstoppable Success in Any Economy: The 7 Divine Mantras to Maximize Your Leadership Potential*
3. *Win the Leadership Game Every Time: Nine Invaluable Laws to Magnify Your Success*

Part 1

How to Become the Leader You Want to Be

1

Define Your Top

At every conference that I speak and in every boardroom where I do team coaching, I ask the participants to write their Professional Aspiration Statement (P.A.S.) in one clear sentence. This chapter is the book's foundation as it emphasizes that you cannot reach the top if you have no idea what your deep professional aspiration looks like.

And so, before you dig further into this book, I would like you to take a moment and write your Professional Aspiration Statement (P.A.S.) in one clear sentence.

And let me warn you, almost ninety percent of the leaders do not know their P.A.S. They confuse their P.A.S. with their goals.

During my coaching sessions and workshops, when I ask people to think and write their P.A.S., most often people immediately take a pencil and paper and begin writing. You would feel like they are absolutely sure of their P.A.S. But when I ask them to read aloud what they have written, I hear their goals. It's not a Professional Aspiration Statement.

You see, my friend, a P.A.S. is unique and more extensive than a goal. A goal is something you set to achieve in the near future. Your P.A.S. is bigger, purposeful, and more defined and shows you the end.

For example, people tell me their P.A.S. is to become a senior Vice President in their company. Well, that's not a P.A.S. It's a goal, a step toward something more purposeful and significant that you want to achieve. Getting to the Vice President's position is a step toward the P.A.S.

Take, for instance, a client who, during the first coaching session, told me that his P.A.S. is to become the company director. I knew that that was not what he truly aspired to become. Now, don't ask me how I knew that.

DOI: 10.4324/9781003439134-2

This, my friend, comes with years of coaching people across industries and countries.

So, I took time with him, and in every coaching session, I helped him to become more aware of and identify his genuine professional aspirations. I worked with him on deriving his P.A.S. After a few months, he told me that his true aspiration was to become the C.E.O. of a company that focused on giving back to society. It was then that he understood that becoming a company director was only a step toward his P.A.S.

In yet another instance, my client wrote that her P.A.S. was to be an impactful leader and get to the next level. Well, that's a generalized goal. After taking her through the P.A.S. process, it turned out her P.A.S. was to get recognized as a Telecom Industry leader and transform the field. Now that's bigger and more purposeful.

Why do I encourage everyone to define their P.A.S.? Why do I not go ahead with the coaching process unless I have people identify their P.A.S.? Because we are in a world where people more often give up on their dreams than fulfilll them.

Your P.A.S. is the top to where you want to reach. It's what getting to the top means for you as an individual. And if you are unclear about your P.A.S., you will stay lost in the corporate web. A web we weave for ourselves, always looking for something outside. Many of us are stuck in this web hopping from one company to another, searching for growth and fulfillment, only to realize in the end that we did not achieve what we truly wanted in our career lives.

Those who clearly define their top, their P.A.S., work toward a bigger purpose. Rarely do they feel unfulfilled, and rarely do these people give up. Such people who have a clear definition of P.A.S. are the ones who stay on track, they say no when needed, they make the right decisions about their career, and feel energetic to move ahead. You want to be one of them.

You see my friend, goals are often centered on the short term or the near future. Aspirations are much more future-focused and deep-rooted in purpose.

In the epic Indian tale of the Ramayana, Lord Ram emerges not only as a divine figure but also as a beacon of wisdom, offering valuable lessons that extend beyond the spiritual realm to various facets of life, particularly P.A.S. Fighting Ravan and freeing Sita were goals but the P.A.S. was Ram's unwavering commitment to righteousness (dharma), which formed the cornerstone of his life.

Once you identify your P.A.S., then you begin to chunk it down in layers, and that's when you arrive at a vision, a goal, and subgoals that determine your action plan.

As an analogy, think of a tree. A tree's visible, beautiful parts are its branches, leaves, flowers, and fruits, and one is tempted to nurture and water them. But the unseen roots are the foundation; without the root, there is no branch or fruit. If you want the tree of your career to bloom, you need to take care of the roots. Your P.A.S. is that root that needs to be nurtured because it will determine the type of career tree you will grow into.

Have you seen how some people have a great start in their career and you feel their career is going to blossom? Meet them after twelve years of their career. Their career tree will look withered. They are confused and face mid-life career syndrome where they feel they want to do more, but don't know what to do. And this happens even with senior leaders after they reach a high position only to wonder if that's what they truly wanted.

And so P.A.S. is your foundation, which you must start working on early in your career and keep it evolving throughout your career.

My father often told me you can add several floors to a building if the foundation is strong. The P.A.S. is our foundation for building a great career and staying on course. That's how you get to the top.

Your P.A.S. is something that makes you complete from the inside. It brings you a sense of stability, calmness, and happiness, as seen through your facial expression. Almost anyone who has worked with me and has been able to define their P.A.S. experiences a sense of fulfillment and peace in them. They believe they know what they are here for. They work with clarity and know when and whom to say yes to.

Now don't confuse P.A.S. with passion.

Twenty years back, when I stepped into corporate America, one word that awed me was "Passion."

Until then, I hadn't heard the word this many times. "Follow your passion," "Follow your dreams," said personal development gurus. As an executive coach, I have witnessed this very word *passion* contribute to more business and career failures than success. Statements like "follow your passion" or "first know what you are most passionate about," "jump into it," or "find a job that matches it," goodness God!

These are perilous pieces of advice from motivational gurus, professional coaches, and bloggers.

Well, no offense! But this hypothesis is unsuitable for anyone's career journey. Many who come to me for coaching hope to follow their passion. They're always taken aback when I tell them that following their passion isn't a path. I see countless aspiring leaders led astray by such advice because they spend hours and months trying to figure out what they are most passionate about and then take a leap to move toward their passion, only to fail later.

Being associated with some of the most successful leaders in the world, I've learned from them that there's more to their story than just passion.

Their passion is a blend of the following:

Intention + Effort + Focus + Clarity + BluePrint + Awareness + Commitment

The business world then labels it a passion with all the invisible ingredients which most of us don't see. So focus more on your P.A.S. and define it clearly.

YOU CAN DEFINE YOUR P.A.S. IN THREE SIMPLE STEPS

Step #1: For the next three days, constantly think of that one thing you truly desire to achieve before you leave your professional life forever. Do this by asking yourself the following question many times a day for the next three days: "If there were one thing I would want to achieve before I say goodbye to my professional life, what would that one thing be?"

Step #2: Observe if your response stays the same for the three days whenever you ask yourself the above question.

Step #3: To ensure your P.A.S. is not a fad and is something you truly want to achieve, ask yourself, "If I do not achieve this, would it completely break me from the inside, and would I feel unfulfilled in my professional life?" If the answer to this question is a yes, your P.A.S. is true. If the answer to the above question is a no, you still need clarification about your true P.A.S.

Defining your P.A.S. is the most critical and complex step in your career. Once you know what your P.A.S. looks like, you have defined what top looks like for you and will know when you reach there.

How you approach opportunities and position yourself is just as impactful as how hard you work or what technical skills you develop. Most of us when we get "stuck" in our career, either look for an opportunity outside our current company or we stay and begin blaming the people and circumstances around us for limiting our ability to grow. But what if there's a third way? What if instead of leaving or becoming bitter, you could identify what you really want to achieve and discover the deeper why.

Making it to the top, my friend, is no rocket science. Everyone can get there. What matters is knowing what the top looks like for you. Otherwise, you will be like Alice in Wonderland, where one day when the cat asks Alice, "Where are you going?" Alice responds by asking, "Which way should I go?" The cat says, "That depends on where you are going." Alice says, "I don't know." The cat looks at Alice in amusement and says "then it doesn't matter which way you go."

NASA made it to the moon because the moon was the destination they wanted to reach. When you know where you want to reach, the how becomes easy. You have to know what you want, the how will follow.

I often encourage both my daughters, who are on their journey to success, to be clear on their P.A.S. because not having a direction, not knowing where you are going, can get you nowhere.

You go nowhere. You can never get "there," and can never arrive anywhere, because you don't have a destination. And that's when you will be pulled in all directions and you will settle for whatever comes your way. And I know you are here with this book in your hand to play big in your career life and achieve great heights.

You want to reach to your top and you and I both know that you can and you will. Just hold on to your P.A.S.

REFLECT

Think on these two questions and then draft your one-liner P.A.S.

1. *Where do you want to reach?*
2. *What does the top look like for you?*

2

Sustain at the Top

Sanjay, a high-achieving leader at a technology company who graduated from an Ivy League university, was recently promoted to the C.E.O. role. Despite his achievements and apparent aptitude, Sanjay worries that he needs to be more knowledgeable to lead the organization effectively. This constant self-sabotage has led to stress, because of which he is facing insomnia.

Then there's Maria – an accomplished C.E.O of an advertising firm in Las Vegas. Maria's life now is all about traveling in a private jet, being alone most of the time, and having to deliver results to the shareholders. These days, there is so much tension in her body, causing her to get irritated at the slightest issue and make irrational decisions, not to mention some unethical behaviors she's been accused of.

Chris is the Managing Director of a well-known firm headquartered in India. Chris handles the company's North American operation out of its Dallas office. Before transitioning into this role, Chris was known as an anti-fragile leader, extremely popular amongst his people. These days, however, he is rude to his people, has become less charismatic, and gets angry at the slightest issues. His stress has led to high blood pressure problems for him.

What's going on here? Why are high-potential leaders not able to deliver outstanding results?

It's because many of us forget to keep working on ourselves after making it to the top. Sustaining at the top is more important than reaching to the top.

It will require you to put more effort into sustaining your success than simply reaching there. Most people fail at this level. They find it easy to start and difficult to sustain.

DOI: 10.4324/9781003439134-3

Sustaining at the top requires a different approach. You cannot sustain at the top by being the same person with the same behaviors that brought you to the top. The main lesson I've learned along the way is that what makes you successful right now won't always guarantee success over the long term.

One of the questions I often ask my audience is this: What would a 3.0 version of you look like? I am always amazed at the responses I get. Here are a few:

1. I want to see myself in a good position.
2. I see myself with more knowledge and skills where I can make decisions.
3. I want to be a mentor.
4. I see someone who can focus on team development.
5. I will be a leader who can nurture the next set of leaders.
6. I would shift focus from "Doing things" to "Getting things done."
7. I will be financially strong.
8. I want to achieve a C.E.O. position.
9. I will position myself as a strategic leader ready to bring about change.
10. I would be starting my business as an I.T. consultant.
11. I will be making a significant impact in the learning and development sector.
12. I would be the managing director of this very company.
13. I will lead the company to its next level.
14. I would be named the best leader in my industry.

All these sounds so magical. But sadly, most people will not achieve what they want. I say this from twenty-one years of coaching experience.

The reason is that these people will be functional and technical experts at work but will never unleash and use their professional powers to become a meta-leader.

Their powers will be caged behind self-doubt, fear, anger, self-criticism, second-guessing their ideas, fear of what others might think, personal responsibilities, and imposter syndrome, so they will never become the 3.0 version of themselves.

I have seen that most people get stuck in the second version, the 2.0, of their careers.

It is like being stuck in an infinite loop. You go to work, give your best, upskill and reskill yourself, get a slight salary increment or a new position, and then get stuck there for years. You reach your late forties and realize you have little time left in the corporate world. And then you start looking around at what you should do, you lose confidence in yourself, and the next thing you know is that you are dragging yourself to work each day.

Refrain from getting stuck in this loop and focus on how things were in the past. Every next level of your career life will demand a NEW YOU.

THE CORN CROP

One of my good friend and Chief Executive Officer of a start up in Dallas told me an interesting story of a very hardworking farmer committed to his work. He had a young son to whom he decided to teach a practical lesson that would benefit him all through his life.

The farmer gave his son some corn seeds and told him to plant, nurture, grow, and harvest them. Excitedly, his son took the seeds and planted them in the small portion of land his father had prepared for him. He adequately watered the seeds and constantly did all that was needed for the plant to grow. After three weeks of planting and constant care, the corn plant began to bud. And as the days went by, the corn plant continued to grow.

Two months after the planting, the corn cobs were now partially formed. Seeing this, the farmer's son was very excited. He then decided that since the corn plant had already started producing corn cobs, he would no longer look after them but simply wait until the end of the remaining two weeks when they would be due for harvesting. He went on to spend days with his friends and engage in other leisure activities, leaving the corn crops to themselves.

Then the expected day of harvest came, and when he got to the piece of land, he did not find any corn to harvest. Shocked and disappointed, he moved around the ground and discovered that most of the crops had wilted due to a lack of water and plant disease. The ones that managed to grow were eaten by animals, and the other corn stalks were trampled on. There was not a single corn remaining.

Sad and disappointed, he went to his father and told him he had nothing to present. His father, aware of how he had failed to constantly watch over the crop after they started producing cobs, sat him down and counseled him.

He explained that it was not enough that the corn germinated and produced cobs, but he needed to watch over it to the end when it was ripe enough for harvest. He told him of the roaming animals, the weeds, the required nutrients, the plant diseases, and the other conditions that could stop the plant from reaching full maturity – which he needed to guard against.

Similarly, you need to protect your success at all levels so that you won't lose it to harmful factors. Most of us start out with the right mindset, which enables us to take actions that lead to our growth and success. But then our mindset becomes indifferent, and we suffer as our progress slows down. And so, it's important to always keep our thoughts right to take the necessary actions to protect our success.

As you succeed, your success will demand that you grow and change. The more successful you become, the more difficult and painful your journey towards sustaining it will be.

WHAT SUCCESSFUL LEADERS DO TO SUSTAIN SUCCESS?

Most of us sleepwalk through our career life, operating in an autopilot mode. And then we begin to realize that we are failing and then we give up. I fail more than most people. I've had failures in business. I've had failed relationships. And I used to wonder why this happened to me all the time. I began playing a victim. But as my career progressed, I realized that failures are the price we pay for success. Failures stretch us and help us sustain success.

Too many of us live and work in what I call the safe comfort zone. Same work for the past twenty years. The same drive to perform. Same conversations. Same skills. Once you use your powers and rise to the state of a meta-leader, you will feel the old everyday self was a sleepwalker, barely conscious of their limitless potential.

Some of the most successful leaders I have worked with have learned to sustain their success by welcoming change, accelerating their learning, self-reflection, developing emotional maturity, maintaining discipline, working harder than before, and continuously working on becoming the best version of themselves.

Most successful leaders know that staying at the top is more critical than only reaching the top. It will demand more from you. I have seen many leaders make it to the top and then slide down the slippery road. And this usually happens because we often believe that we will continue to be successful once we have succeeded. And we use the same old methods rather than adapting to new ones.

Many people tell me they want to be successful. And I tell them it's not enough to be successful. You want to be successful again and again and again and again and again. You want to sustain success and always have a competitive edge.

So go ahead, stretch today. Ask for what you want. Do things differently. Begin to use your underutilized powers. Do it.

A few days back, I was reading about the Industrial Revolution in Europe when I came across the story of "knocker-uppers." Before alarm clocks existed, the job of waking people up was done by "human alarm clocks," people known as knocker-ups or knocker-uppers. They roamed the city streets in the early morning hours tapping on windows to wake their clients from slumber so they could get to work on time. Many of them worked hard. I'm sure they worked smart too – with well-balanced, aerodynamic and sonorous sticks. Still, they lost their livelihoods in a jiffy when alarm clocks came into the market. This may remind you of the plight of typists. Once considered a well-remunerated high skill job, typists vanished as computers became ubiquitous.

What are the skills that you should be investing in, in order to stay ahead of the curve? Are you watering yourself daily with continuous learning? Are you spending time learning to do things that can't be done by every average person in your field?

Are you learning skills for which you can charge a premium? If you focus merely on doing the minimum, doing what everyone else does, not investing in learning the skills of the future, you will slip down the success ladder. What are the specialized skills that you can develop that could double your income in the next 12 months? I bet there would be something. Only if you stop and take time to look around!

REFLECT

How are you bringing about a change in yourself to help you sustain your success?

3

The Future Is of a Meta-Leader

Most people in the corporate world get stuck at the mid-level or senior level. And when I use the word stuck, I don't just mean hierarchical. Some get stuck in the hierarchy, others do the same job in the same role for years, and many more get stuck in growing out of their job and doing something more significant.

In all of my public appearances on stage, I often ask people to raise their hands if they want to achieve something big in their professional lives and if they want to make a difference. By and large, almost everyone in the room raises their hand, which tells me we all have a deep-seated desire to play big in our career lives. The problem is, we don't know how to get there.

The business world has made us believe that success, growth, promotion, and visibility happen purely because of hardwork and effort.

Ask any achiever the secret of their success, and you will likely get the answer, "Well, I worked hard, had the right credentials, education, and experience, and just happened to be at the right place at the right time." Let me tell you, this is true, but not the whole absolute brutal truth.

I've learned the whole absolute brutal truth by being associated with and studying some of the world's most prominent and well-known leaders. And the whole absolute brutal truth is that these people whom you see standing head and shoulders above others, in reality, work harder on themselves than on their job.

They do things that differ from what you hear or read about them. They consciously transform themselves to be a better leader. They align the outer and inner leadership powers that allow them to go beyond their limitations and concepts created by their mind to realize their full potential.

I call these leaders meta-leaders. These leaders dare to bridge the gap between where they are and where they want to be.

DOI: 10.4324/9781003439134-4

However, being a meta-leader isn't science fiction and is certainly not about being a superhero. To be a meta-leader means to move past the limitations constructed by the mind and enter a new state of awareness where we have deliberate and concrete access to peak experiences that can transform people's lives from the inside out.

Meta-leaders work harder on themselves than they work on their job.

Meta-leaders are highly self-aware about their leadership powers and can see things from a higher perspective.

If you look closely at your work life, you will realize that to achieve your career dream it matters less how smart you are, what potential you have, how skilled you are, how much innate talent you are born with, or where you come from.

Sure, these are important, but they mean little if you do not know how to leverage your professional powers for your growth and your organization's success.

And to align these powers, you must get the conscious mind out of your way, so that the rest of your consciousness can communicate its knowledge. This is how the meta-leader accomplishes what they do.

There are leaders whose scope of thinking, influence, and accomplishment extends far beyond their formal or expected bounds of authority.

A meta-leader is someone who, through their conscious mind, taps into the powers of their leadership as it relates to influence, instincts, moods, attributes, position, emotions, feelings, and habits.

People admire a meta-leader. They seem to be better than anyone else around. They appear super busy, yet consistently find the time for a friend or associate who needs advice.

They have a deep-end purpose. Regardless of how many hours they've worked a day or week, a meta-leader always seems energized. Somehow, they always seem fit, both mentally and physically.

These are the breed of leaders in whom there is no obsession, no disorganization, no conflicts, and no emotional instability. They have emotional mastery. They have a harmonious relationship with themselves and with nature.

Do such leaders even exist? Yes, they do. But the numbers are low.

To name a few, Mahatma Gandhi, Nelson Mandela, Mother Teresa, Rabindranath Tagore, Warren Buffet, and Dhirubhai Ambani, among others.

If you pick up and read the biographies of any of these leaders, you will find one thing in common: they all relied on their professional powers.

I've worked with some of the meta-leaders in real life.

One is Rohan, the senior vice president, whom I met while delivering a leadership session in his company in Bangalore, India. Rohan wants to bring about a change in the way hiring and business are done in the manufacturing firm. When he first shared his idea of inclusion with his company, no one showed any interest. The company had a particular hiring policy that was practiced for years, and they hated anyone outside the company joining leadership roles. These so-called "outsiders" were not welcomed well in the company and were often left aside, feeling lonely and alone, ultimately resigning.

Rohan did not give up. For nine years, he continued pushing his ideas and thoughts on diversifying the hiring process. His boss condemned him on many occasions. But Rohan persisted with his idea. And finally, in 2018, one year before his retirement, the company had a new C.E.O., and he promoted Rohan's idea of diversified hiring. To achieve this level of sustainability, Rohan had worked on making himself a meta-leader and aligning his leadership powers.

In yet another incident, Tom worked as a manager at a food manufacturing company in Oklahoma City. He made lunch meat. In his off-hours, he liked to do crossword puzzles. He got very good at it. He was so good that he started creating his own when he ran out of puzzles. Then, he became so skilled at creating new puzzles that he began selling them. That was decades ago. Today, if you want one of the best books on the subject, pick up a copy of *The New York Times Crossword Puzzle Dictionary*—by Tom Pulliam.

Oh, yes, Tom also made a name (and a fortune) for himself as an actor, doing voiceovers for a wide range of TV and radio commercials. Tom would insist that he was no more intelligent than the next guy. Maybe not, but he definitely took a cue from Albert Einstein, who advised that we should live out of our imagination rather than out of our memory.

During America's recession in 2008, Maria lost her job as an IT cloud manager. Being a single parent, Maria had to feed herself and her two-year-old son Jake. While others around her were tensed and began taking up any job, Maria made a difficult decision. She decided to go her own way and started offering consulting services to start-ups and supporting their IT department.

At first, she'd do it for small amounts of money and sometimes even free.

As she advanced in her skills and reputation, she began earning more and more money. After a decade, she had entirely replaced her income (and then some) with her new career. Maria did what very few of us would do. She began leveraging her nights and weekends to build her new side gig because she knew it takes the risk out of the enterprise until you're ready.

A mature woman led some IT-related teams, including some "difficult technicians" who were remotely located and often disengaged in team meetings. She made a 180-degree shift over a few months. She described herself as a "task-focused leader" – the only time she came out of her office was to fix something wrong. She was often surly, and no one liked her. She realized she needed to leave her office and get to know her people better. She made this change quickly – talking to people about what is happening for them, not solely work issues, sharing her problems and mistakes, and starting meetings to discuss positive achievements. She saw significant changes in the team's mood and productivity improvements. One of her critical reflections was that "it is interesting to see that through changing ourselves, we can also change others."

All of them are ordinary individuals who gradually transformed themselves and their thinking to become meta-leaders. Meta-leaders are regular individuals who commit to doing extraordinary things.

One night, over dinner, I had an interesting conversation with a military leader.

Here's what I learned: We can all get better if we are willing to look at ourselves hard.

Can you think of meta-leaders you know of in your life? They may be someone you've read about or someone you work with.

A meta-leader is someone who has the power to become anything they want to. A meta-leader can move past the limitations constructed by the mind and enter a new state of awareness where we have deliberate and concrete access to peak experiences that can transform our life from the inside out.

A meta-leader is anyone who can maximize and utilize the two professional powers, no matter the origins. They have controlled attention, are resourceful, and can persistently overcome challenges and obstacles. They often think and perform differently.

Meta-leaders are grounded in *who* they are and *why* they are leading. Their authenticity rallies those who follow.

They are the ones who exhibit emotional intelligence – self-awareness, self-regulation, and self-motivation.

TABLE 3.1

Qualities of a Meta-Leader

Meta-Leader Qualities
Have the courage to bridge the gap between where they are and where they want to be.
Move past the limitations constructed by the mind.
Enter a new state of awareness.
Can see things from a higher perspective.
Scope of thinking, influence, and accomplishment extends far beyond their formal or expected bounds of authority.
They seem super busy, yet consistently find the time for a friend or associate who needs advice.
They have a deep-end purpose.
Always seems energized.
Have emotional mastery.
They have a harmonious relationship with themselves and with nature.
Fit, both mentally and physically.
Foster this discipline and balance in themselves and others.
Have emotional mastery. They have a harmonious relationship with themselves and with nature.
Have controlled attention, are resourceful, and can persistently overcome challenges and obstacles.
Grounded in *who* they are and *why* they are leading.
Exhibit emotional intelligence – self-awareness, self-regulation, and self-motivation.

In stressful times, they can get up and out of the "basement," the primal survival fear instincts of their brain that otherwise overcomes rational decisions and actions. They foster this discipline and balance in themselves and others.

The world demands that we give it our best. You can't inspire others unless you feel motivated. It's not easy, but also not impossible. To change, one should focus not on fighting the old but on building the new you.

REFLECT

Which qualities of a meta-leader have you developed in you? Choose from the table. I encourage you to reflect on these qualities, check which ones you already possess, and circle the ones you want to challenge yourself to develop.

4

Unleash the Meta-Leader from Within

I've been asked this question numerous times during coaching and workshops on becoming a meta-leader. And when I tell them you already are a meta-leader, they stare into my soul and curiously ask, "Well, why then am I not achieving what I want in my career?" "Why am I not at the Top in my field of work?" Some even laugh and dismiss me when I tell them everyone is a meta-leader.

We don't believe we are meta-leaders because we have never tapped into our powers. And so, we never use our power at work.

Through years of coaching senior leaders and C.E.O.s of Fortune 500 companies, I've realized that we often know what we want to achieve in our careers. We all have the potential to take ourselves, our teams, and our organization to the highest level we can imagine.

Yet, data shows that only 7% of the 3.6 billion workforce achieves great success. The majority are working hard, putting in the effort, and yet needing help to accomplish what they desire. There is a vast gap today in the corporate world between those who succeed and those who don't. There is a gap between you and your greatness.

The majority of people will leave the corporate world feeling used and unfulfilled. Sadly, they would have never made full use of their leadership powers.

Success has nothing to do with the right timing, your potential, and your talent. It has everything to do with how you transform your thinking and behaviors in ways that you can achieve infinite possibilities.

As an executive coach, I often have to remind my clients how powerful they are and how they can exercise that power. Because in the day-to-day grind of our work, we usually operate in an autopilot zone and stop unleashing the daily powers that can help us step into our greatness.

DOI: 10.4324/9781003439134-5

When faced with adversity, a leader's capacity to identify and execute the professional powers to help the team and the organization grow is the most crucial element of leadership.

For leaders to succeed in the new era of business that will transcend the physical world into the metaverse, they must work massively on themselves more than their jobs. Leaders who transform and evolve can significantly impact and benefit people and organizations.

Look at the millions of people who shy away from owning their professional powers.

Personally, I've had some good seasons and some painful ones in my career. I've made some spectacularly good choices and some outrageously bad mistakes. And each day, even now, I think of myself as a leader who is a work in progress.

The same applies to you. Now, you might be saying, "I can't do all the things Payal does. It's easy for her. She is a transformation guru. It's easy for her." Well, sorry to disappoint you. Nope. It's not easy for me. I am no different than you. Each day, I have my struggles, fears, frustrations, hopes, and dreams, working each day on myself to become a better version of myself.

I don't always get it right. But I try so hard to unleash the meta-leader in me. Because I know that life will send you and me many windows of opportunity each day, and where you reach in your career will ultimately be decided by how you respond to these daily opportunities.

And to reach the Top, you have to play big by unleashing the meta-leader within you.

Let me be upfront and tell you something here. I've been in the people transformation business for over 21 years. Transformation is hardwork. And because it is hard, many leave it mid-way.

It's not that you get out of bed one day and say, "Today, I am going to make it to the top." Getting to the Top in your field of work is transforming yourself into one. And transformation is a continuous process. It's a daily process. It happens each day. It's not something we learn once and have forever.

And so, why do we have few people at the Top? Well, that's because to be at the Top, you've got to put in the hardwork and work on yourself. And in today's workforce generation, no one has the time to do this.

There is a grandfather clock at my mom's home. It's more than 75 years old. The clock has a long pendulum, and every stroke makes you feel at rest, saying there is plenty of time. Look at our modern-day clock. With a shorter, thinner pendulum, it seems to tell time is running out.

Everything is speeding up in our modern corporate world, so most people are grinding. Where is the time to become a meta-leader and unleash your powers?

Through this book, I will guide you by unleashing a meta-leader inside of you by practicing and applying the powers you possess as a leader each day. I will help you identify the powers and harness them.

You possess the most incredible machine ever invented, so extraordinary that only a higher power could create it. And that incredible, extraordinary machine is your brain, a nervous system, and the ineffable human mind. And even more exciting is that you are this machine's owner and operator.

While coaching numerous leaders and C.E.O.s globally, my most significant discovery is that the secret to success is obvious, yet it isn't seen. And even if people become enlightened with this secret, the needed effort holds most people back from doing anything significant in their lives.

Who doesn't love armchair quarterbacking on a Sunday afternoon, watching Netflix, or playing a football game? Most people will spend 30–40– years of their working life going to work, working hard, earning a good salary, and relaxing over the weekend.

If you want to achieve something remarkable, you must transform yourself into a meta-leader, aligning the mind, body, behavior, and soul. This book will serve as a guide for you to align your inner and outer leadership powers. If you are stuck in your career, this book will help you get unstuck if you promise to consistently work on the four leadership powers.

Reach to the Top is a book about you, me, and everyone wanting to succeed. It tells you that you can unleash the meta-leader. The book is a guide to help you get access to your powers and the infinite potential you have to achieve extraordinary things for yourself, the team, and the organization.

This book is what everyone needs today if they are going to succeed. If you want to be at the Top of your game and enjoy life how you want it to be, you need to recognize your powers and unleash the meta-leader. Because, ultimately, leadership is a power game.

REFLECT

Am I ready and committed to bringing about a transformation in myself to unleash the meta-leader within?

5

It Takes More Than Performance

"Power resides only where men believe it resides, and it's on us to use our powers," is a statement I would often hear from Lewis, the C.E.O. of a well-known mid-size financial company I worked for in the early years of my career.

He would often repeat this quote in all of his speeches. In those early years of my job, I didn't quite understand what he meant by this. And honestly, I was not bothered much about it either.

After a few years, I resigned from this company to step out of corporate America to start my coaching and training firm. This company has a tradition that when anyone resigns, they meet with Mr Lewis, the company's C.E.O., before leaving. I found it an interesting concept. I prepared a thank you speech without knowing what to expect at this meeting.

As I thanked him for my time here with the company and spoke about my new entrepreneurial journey, Lewis said the exact quote I had heard a hundred times.

He said, "Payal, remember this always, 'power resides only where men believe it resides, and it's on us to use our powers." I smiled and nodded my head in affirmation. After a few more discussions, I happily took his leave, enthusiastically looking ahead to my future career journey.

I began setting up my firm, and in every failure, in every success, for some reason, Lewis's statement, "power resides only where men believe it resides, and it's on us to use our powers," stayed with me. With every setback and opportunity, my belief in this statement grew, and I began to understand its deep meaning. I understood that to reach the top takes more than performance and hardwork.

I traveled worldwide, being invited to speak at conferences and summits.

At one such conference in Mumbai, India, where I was the keynote speaker, I was seated at a table doing a book signing for the audience after my session.

By lunch, I had completed signing all 175 copies of my book, *Success Is Within*. During lunch, I grabbed some of my favorite Indian vegetarian dishes from the buffet.

As I settled down to eat the delicious Indian meal, a gentleman wearing a suit with neatly combed hair and a pair of eyeglasses walked up to me, introduced himself as a senior director at a well-known IT company, and asked, "May I sit here and talk to you about a matter of importance to me?"

I smiled and welcomed him to have lunch with me.

As we were eating, he directly broached his problems and said,

> Payal, I am fifty-three years old with over twenty years of experience; I am near retirement, and yet I am simply not where I want to be in my career. I gave all of my time and energy to managing projects and deadlines, achieving goals and targets for the company, and balancing family life. I became the senior director and felt that was a success for me.
>
> But today, when you spoke about the meta-leader and how we can achieve infinite possibilities for ourselves, our teams, and our organizations, I realized I've not even used a fraction of my powers. I could've achieved more than position, title, goals, and targets. But I want to change that now for whatever time I have left. I want to do something bigger and better with your coaching help.

In yet another incident, while conducting a workshop on "Win The Leadership Game" for the senior leaders and functional heads at a company in Silicon Valley of India, Bangalore, many of these leaders shared with me how they lack confidence in their ability to make decisions. They have the power, status quo, and knowledge but aren't reaching the top.

One of their senior leaders told me, "Payal, I think most of us do not use our powers to scale up and grow."

A few months back, I was in Milpitas, California, conducting the same workshop for senior executives. We were all sitting at a huge round table during lunch, and it was easy to see and talk with each other. One of the things that came out big time was the need to play big and maximize their potential. And I again noticed how these leaders needed to use their leadership powers.

Everyone today is working hard to improve their performance. Performance doesn't guarantee success. In fact, many a times good performance can hurt your progress because you become so indispensable to the role that your boss might be unwilling to do anything for your growth because of the fear of losing you from that role.

Great performance itself is insufficient without the use of your leadership powers.

Now let me share with you something interesting here.

Before every corporate workshop that I conduct, my team sends the participants a pre-questionnaire for me to assess their mindset, behaviors, and challenges. When I often ask them about their biggest leadership challenge, my typical response is that I cannot utilize my full potential.

This challenge is faced by all, from managers and senior leaders to C.X.O.s of companies, the organization's group with access to the best resources and knowledge.

Why are high-performing individuals who are working hard facing potential maximization challenges?

People worldwide are working on maximizing their potential but often need to catch up; the scriptures say we can move mountains, yet we need to be closer to achieving success in our daily work lives. Why is this so?

Because more than potential and hardwork, making it to the top is a power game, and we fail to utilize our professional powers, which we are so fortunate to be blessed with. Every leader has powers and must know how to use the powers and when to exploit their powers.

All of us have the power to achieve infinite possibilities. Few of us believe in our powers and use them.

Most of us don't believe we have the power; even if we do, we tend to shy away from using it. Most of us think other people and situations have more power than us.

Rather than being down on ourselves and focusing on our flaws, what would happen if we were to be as bold all through the day and say, "I am unique. I am wonderful. I am valuable."

Leadership is ultimately a power game. And when you learn how to unleash and leverage your powers, making it to the top is possible.

In comics and films, powers symbolize a deep inner quality or desired human strength. In reality, your leadership powers are your *traits, experiences, and behaviors, which, when tapped into, will help you to achieve limitless growth for yourself and your organization.*

One of my coaching clients gave me a beautiful book on my birthday titled, *Oh the Places You'll Go'* by Dr Suess. The book's core message is that you have feet in your shoes. You can steer yourself in any direction you choose.

My friend, the wealthiest place on earth today is the graveyard where people take their dreams with them. Through this book, I encourage you to make sure you begin to work toward fulfilling those dreams.

Most people give away their powers to everyone around them. They become remote-controlled, giving the remote of their decision-making to others. And then they blame discrimination and society for their failures.

As you will read in the following pages, life has certainly tested me, and I have failed many of these tests.

Though the corporate and business world calls me a leadership guru, I don't have all the answers. No one does. And if someone out there tells you they have a few easy steps, hacks, and tools to help you succeed at your work, that person is trying to sell you real estate on the San Andreas Fault.

I want you to make a choice today to take charge of your professional powers. I want you to know deep down that you are worth it.

I also want to remind you that the clock is ticking for each of us. The moments that you have left in your career life are ticking down.

No one knows what tomorrow will bring and if you will have this opportunity to use your professional powers to reach the top. So, as long as you are here, use your inner and outer leadership powers to the fullest to achieve success for yourself, your team, your organization, and the world at large. You have incredible powers within you.

We all have dreams. You need a process and a framework to execute your dreams and turn them into reality. In Japanese, this is called Shikumi. It means system-based transformation. When you pair your dream with Shikumi, you become a meta-leader and may reach even the most extraordinary goals.

The business world is transforming faster with the onset of the internet, and everyone is talking about the next major industry transformation. My question is, what will the new leader transformation look like? In times of significant change, bringing about a faster transformation in the self and becoming a meta-leader is paramount. And for his transformation in you to happen quickly, you need Shikumi.

I hope that his book helps you realize your dreams. In this book are the powers you will need to reach the top.

REFLECT

What are some of the inner and outer powers I have used at my work?

Part 2

Using Your Leadership Powers

Power 1

Great Leaders Are Mind Readers

"You have to have big ears and a small mouth. The rule at the top is that the less you speak, the better you are understood." It's a piece of advice I got from a shrewd businessman, which I will never forget.

If you've heard my podcast, it's called *The Payal Nanjiani Leadership Podcast* (rated in the top 10% in the business world); there's a segment in this podcast called "The Iconic," released every Friday, where I have one-on-one candid conversations with the best thought leaders in the corporate world. These include C.E.O.s and executive directors of companies, spiritual gurus, and political leaders.

At the end of the conversation, before we wrap up, there is a rapid-fire leadership segment, where my guests have to respond instantly and blurt out the first answer that comes to mind. There are six questions, out of which one question is this: Which superpower would you choose – invisibility or mind reading?

And I am not surprised that eight out of the ten choose invisibility. Why?

Because they already use their power of mind reading. People who have reached the top have mastered the art of mind reading.

While I was on a business trip to Mexico to do a group coaching for their senior leaders, I got the opportunity to accompany Daniel, the C.E.O. of the automobile company, and his 11-member senior leadership team to a two-day strategic planning meeting planned at Chichén Itzá; I got to see the complex of Mayan ruins and the massive step pyramid, considered one of the world's seven wonders. The whole experience was terrific.

On the way back to the airport, I noticed how the entire team was energetic and full of life, and each said they had always wanted to visit a place like this. I thought, "What planning Daniel might have done to get everyone's opinion on the place and how the whole experience should be."

DOI: 10.4324/9781003439134-8

As we got off the bus at the airport to take our flights back home, Daniel thanked me for my group coaching for his leaders at the company headquarters and for accompanying them to their strategic planning meeting.

But then he said something that startled me. He said, "Thanks for joining Payal at such short notice. I knew you were keen to see a complex of Mayan ruins." Oh boy, he was so right. I wanted to visit Chichén Itzá.

Throughout the flight, one thought that was playing on my mind was, "How did Daniel know that? How I secretly wished I could be a part of this beautiful meeting they've planned at Chichén Itzá?"

After a few days, I spoke with Daniel to update him about his team members' coaching sessions. Before we wrapped up our conversation, I told him, "Daniel, I have two questions for you."

I could sense Daniel's smile as he replied, "I know, Payal; what the one question is?" I stared into the phone while he continued, "You want to know how I gauged that you were thinking of being a part of this planning meeting? Am I correct?"

I stammered while saying yes to him.

"What's the second question then?" he asked. "Well," I said hesitantly, "How did you get all of your team's consensus for the place?" "Oh, let me answer both of your questions together for you," he said. "I did not go in for any consensus. There is no time on my daily calendar to go in for consensus. But I knew that my team was thinking of a place like Chichén Itzá, so I went ahead and asked my executive admin, Carla, to go ahead with the planning. When Carla spoke with the team about the location, everyone said yes. Just like I knew you were thinking of joining in, too. Payal, am I not a great mind reader?" he said humorously.

Wow, I thought to myself when he used the word mind reading. I found it very intriguing.

It's true, my friend. All successful leaders are great mind readers.

Though they, like Daniel, humorously talk about mind reading, I have seen this trait across all who have made it to the top and sustained their success.

Not long ago, I was having dinner at the Taj with the managing director of a company in Mumbai, India. After dinner, I glanced at various cake displays while walking toward the main gate for our respective cars. He asked me, "Do you want to pick these for your two girls?" He was so spot on. I was thinking of picking up a few cakes for the girls.

Time and again, I have been amazed at how these leaders can gauge your thinking. It's a skill I have learned well from them.

Mind reading is a leadership power only a few have unleashed and used.

These few leaders have developed the ability to know what's happening inside the heads of their teams, external stakeholders, board members, and the people around them.

One of the things that these leaders have realized is that it's highly crucial to building the chemistry of the mind.

Most of us have learned well how to build a team. We take our teams out over dinner, offsites, and happy hour evenings to create deep bonding. We are there at their sports events and voluntary activities.

The most amusing part is that at work, these are the same leaders frustrated with their team's performance, with quiet quitting attitudes and sudden resignations.

Those who have made it to the top are the ones who have connected with the minds of their people. They know exactly what triggers their people, their pain points, and what makes them click. They can influence people and connect with them.

I am convinced, more than ever, that a great leader can connect with people, and connecting is all about mind reading.

Mind reading is your ability to identify with people and relate to them in ways that increase your influence on them.

Why is the art of mind reading critical? Because it builds long-lasting, deep, and purposeful relations. It is the single-most crucial element of making it to the top.

I have coached numerous leaders across the globe. I have seen how, even with the best skills, hardwork, and talents, they cannot grow in the company.

For instance, Robert and Daniel are two strong candidates for a Chicago manufacturing firm's Chief Executive Officer role. Both were experts in their field, had been in the company for more than seventeen years, and had excellent skills and abilities under their belt. Between the two of them, Daniel became the Chief Executive Officer. Reason?

The board of directors invited Robert and Daniel to do a presentation about the company and its vision and address this to a staff of 2,050 employees, both on-site and virtual. During the presentation, Robert brought out some fantastic facts and figures, articulated his vision in some excellent PowerPoint slides, did some storytelling, and took it upon himself to get the organization to the next level. He focused on impressing the audience with all he could do for the organization.

In contrast, Robert was engaged with his audience. He asked them questions and felt their pain points. He got off the stage and spoke to them at the level at which they were seated. He told them how each would partner with him to take the organization to the next level. He was open to sharing his failures and challenges. Whatever he said, the audience supported him. The audience felt connected to him. They thought he was able to read their minds.

Talent is needed to reach the top for any generation of leaders. Hardwork isn't enough. Experience isn't enough. One must exhibit vision (where you are going), pragmatism (what problems are to be solved), trustworthiness (walk the talk), and charisma (connect at a personal level). All these qualities depend heavily upon your ability to connect with people and influence them, which means you should know what's in the mind of your key people.

Leaders who have developed the ability to perceive another's thoughts without the traditional means of communication are the ones we call mind readers. And mind reading doesn't mean you get to "know everything."

I believe nearly anyone can use their leadership power of mind reading and influence people more positively. It did not come naturally, but I learned it from the top executives I connect with regularly.

After coaching and studying numerous leaders across various industries globally, here are my findings.

If you want to reach the top and have an advantage over people, you must know how to be a mind reader. Leaders who have developed this power within them understand their people and know exactly what people want, which makes them great influencers.

These leaders tend to know the right buttons to push to motivate people toward their goals. Because they are so passionate and understanding, it seems they have a gift for inspiring people.

Building this trait of mind reading is easier than you might imagine. You can employ powerful leadership tools and techniques to become a more capable mind reader – and, in turn, a far better leader.

You must create mental models to intuit people's thoughts and feelings effectively. How do you do that? There are three simple steps:

Step 1: Categorize each person into four personality types (Figure P1.1)
The Commander: These are task accomplishers. They love to control and have a competitive spirit. They like giving instructions. They are very

THE COMMANDER	THE THINKER
THE SUPPORTER	THE PARTNER

FIGURE P1.1
Four personality types.

impatient and demanding but disciplined and fast-paced. These are the people who love authority. They could be insensitive toward people. They are primarily transactional in their discussions. They don't believe much in relation-building. However, they build their inner circle with a few who build good relations. They're often so focused on having all the ideas and being right all the time that it can appear like they need to be more willing to listen to others. They don't take criticism well, and they're often inflexible. Commanders are people who are high on task and low on relations.

The Thinker: They are deeply in tune with patterns, data, symbols, and abstract possibilities. They stick to details and gather all the relevant facts before deciding. They aim for too much perfection and love to be right all the time. They are drawn toward novelty and transformation. They're rigorous planners who prepare and stick to a schedule to carry out tasks, deliver on responsibilities, and pursue goals. Self-discipline, self-control, and punctuality come naturally to them. They have strong opinions, and it's hard for them to see someone else's personality. They avoid conflicts and have trouble sharing their thoughts. Thinkers are low on tasks and low on relations.

The Supporter: They try to build connections with their teams and management over dinner meets and happy hours and work toward a consensus. They look around for ways to build relationships and get their way through. Supporters tend to put others' needs ahead of their own. This type of person is highly attuned to others and often seen as agreeable, helpful, and kind, but can also have trouble advocating for themselves. They always need approval and validation from others before doing any task. Supporters are low on task and high on relations.

The Partner: The best leaders care about personality traits because they help them anticipate how they'll interact with others in the workplace.

They believe in building relations and making change happen together. They give feedback. They build trust. They understand people and work with empathy. They are genuinely interested in people. Partners are never afraid to share their learnings, mistakes, and problems. They are vulnerable, and at the same time, they are in control. These are the ones who are game-changers; partners are high on task and high on relations.

Step 2: Understand their triggers
Think about the individuals on your team. What are their likely triggers? How have they responded in the past to different situations? Make a list of the names of people in your team, your external stakeholders, your upper management, and anyone in direct contact or reporting to you.

Now, against each name, pick as many questions you want at a time and begin finding answers to these questions for each individual. Try and pick not more than three questions each time and keep the questions the same for all. By the end of two months, you would have collected some essential data and become a mind-reader.

Here are some questions for you to consider.

What motivates each person?
What are their fears and triggers?
What obstacles are holding them back?
How do they make choices?
Why are they behaving in specific ways?
What do they think about you and the organization?
What drove those actions?
How and why did they think and act that way?
What might they have done to form this behavior?
What habits contributed to her traits that you observed in an incident?

Step 3: Listen and be in the moment
This is one quality I have learned from these leaders. It's one of the most critical of the three steps. The best leaders are so attentive to everything around them. They listen entirely to what you say (and what you don't say), observe everything around them exceptionally well, and speak less while allowing you to do most of the talking. Every opportunity to be around people, make sure you listen and observe thoroughly.

By categorizing people into the four personality types, thinking through what triggers others, and being observant, you can better anticipate their thoughts, feelings, and actions. You will soon begin to speak in the same language as them.

Great leaders are mind readers. They invest more time in people than tasks. They go beyond traditional connecting and networking methods.

Armed with this kind of insight, you can lead far more powerfully because you can say and do the things that resonate most with your team.

While telepathy sounds like a superpower, reading someone's mind is a skill that can be learned. From anticipating a client's needs to knowing how to approach your boss, developing an inner intuition about what others value can help you get ahead.

You have to have big ears and a small mouth. The rule at the top is that the less you speak, the more you are understood.

LEADERSHIP CHALLENGE

Consciously categorize people into the four personality types, understand their motivators, and connect with their heart, mind, and soul.

Power 2

Radiate Positive Relational Energy

Every person who enters the corporate world enters with hopes and dreams to make it big one day. Each of us is bestowed with the ability to succeed. Few of us, however, will make it big in their career.

Researchers have looked for the secret to successful leadership for centuries.

In my work with some top leaders, I've found that the most significant predictor of success for leaders, the secret to their success, is not their charisma or influence. It is not personality, attractiveness, or innovative genius. While we often chew on these pertinent leadership qualities, the one thing that supersedes all these factors is positive relational energy: the energy exchanged between people that helps uplift, enthuse, and renew others. And few leaders generate this power from within and use it to their advantage.

Yui is five feet two inches. She is a petite software engineer from Japan who relocated to the United States of America with her husband and two children in 2001. At that time, Yui was the company's senior manager. I got to know Yui as my neighbor, and we soon became good friends. Daily, we would walk together after dinner. We would talk about many things, from careers to movies to the culture of Japan and India. During one such evening walk, the coach in me came alive, and I asked her what her big career aspiration was. She smiled and said that she aspired to become the company's Chief Information Officer. Little did she know that after seven years of her telling this, she would be the company's Chief Information Officer, but I did not understand the journey would be difficult for her.

Yui faced a lot of criticism and snide remarks for her petite look. People often felt that she needed the charisma and personality to be the Chief

DOI: 10.4324/9781003439134-9

Information Officer, which she lacked. But Yui did not let that hold her back from achieving her career aspiration.

She did something else with hardwork that many of us wouldn't.

Yui had understood early on that her team's performance was critical for her to reach the top. So, she decided to use her relationship energy.

Of the many ways Yui radiated positive relational energy (P.M.E.), one was about reverse psychology to help her change how she looked at the team.

Yui led a team of 35, many of whom were outside of the United States. As luck would have it, many of her team members resisted Yui as a boss as they found her petite and added to it being a woman of color. And so, her team would always complain about anything and everything. They resisted any proposition or idea Yui had. You know, those types of employees who have issues with working hours, project deadlines, internet connection, laptop, cellphone, and even the weather. They remind you of those terrifying creatures called dementors from Harry Potter. As J.K. Rowling describes them, they infest the darkest, filthiest places; they glory in decay and despair; they drain peace, hope, and happiness from the air around them. You might know someone in your workplace who fits this description – they seem to suck all the light and life out of a room.

Yui had many such dementors around her. But rather than behaving negatively with them and ignoring them, she radiated positive relative energy to them.

First, she began to understand their concerns or perspectives by listening and responding supportively. Each morning, she would spend time talking with them and apprehending them. Things got a little better, but her team still resisted her.

They were still pushing back, but Yui stuck with supportive communication despite the understandable temptation to abandon them.

Then, she decided to ask them a question continuously. She asked, "What's the best thing you did for someone today?" This slight shift made all the difference – instead of complaining and resisting, they looked around for opportunities to report their positive impact. It ignited creativity in them and boosted the performance of most of her team members.

Slowly, things got much better, and many of her team members began appreciating her ideas and thoughts. Today, while Yui is the Chief Information Officer, she credits her success to applying positive relational energy, which she still uses in many ways.

What helped Yui was her positive relational energy. It took her and her career to great heights. Yui might not have had the charisma or personality, but she had one of the essential leadership traits: positive relational energy. The performance of any team led by Yui exceeded industry averages by 4X simply by using the power of positive relational energy.

When leaders display positive relational energy, it catapults performance to a new level.

Positive relational energy (P.M.E.) doesn't always refer to simply smiling, looking cheerful, or standing tall with a great personality. It is more about the overall perspective you bring to your workplace.

P.M.E. is your ability to accept that things don't always turn out how you want them to and yet actively and continuously appreciate the good things in your life.

Leaders who practice P.M.E. respond to challenges with a desire for action, healthy vigor, and an upbeat attitude in any circumstance.

Leaders at the top are known to apply this power of P.M.E. in their everyday lives. Managing crises becomes a part of your daily life when you take leadership.

The mood of the leaders can permeate the entire organization. And so you've got to invest your mental and emotional resources in your daily interactions with others.

One of the most influential principles that form the basis of P.M.E. is the Heliotropic Effect, which states that every living system tends to move toward positive energy and away from negative energy.

P.M.E. can be radiated in many ways, enabling you to build a great team and move toward the top.

You could ask an employee to lead a weekly staff meeting on a rotating basis and to present something they specialize in. You can *conduct* regular one-on-one meetings between you and your direct reports. P.M.E. can be generated through gratitude, compassion, trustworthiness, kindness, and forgiveness.

Despite its benefits, most leaders underutilize the power of positive relational energy because we spend more time dwelling on the negative elements of people's relationships than the positive ones. Hence, our behaviors result in the deployment of negative relational energy, which drains our mental energy and impacts our decision-making skills.

Add that you allow situations and people to hijack your emotions, feelings, agenda, day, and actions. You become a remote-controlled leader.

Recently, while coaching a senior director, he told me how his boss came across rudely after his presentation by telling my client that he and his team are always slow in putting things together. My client knew this wasn't a correct observation from his boss, so my client argued back, and that argument wasn't a very healthy one. From that day on, my client has been talking negatively about his boss, which hasn't been conducive to his career. When he heard me speak with him about positive relational energy and how he could radiate that to change his relationships with people for the better, including his boss, things began changing in his career life.

Anyone can effectively use positive relational energy to build better relations and work better with people.

Most of us have energy-draining habits like overthinking, complaining, people-pleasing, living in the past, and poor diet. To begin with, a simple way is to create energy maps to identify positive energizers and the black holes that suck the life out of the system (Figure P2.1).

My work takes me places and allows me to meet executives and leaders across the globe. Most executives appear to have it all together from the outside yet fall short when it concerns their ability to influence their team and drive results. It is said that a significant and challenging part of leadership is managing people. Having worked with thousands of leaders globally, I have understood that the most difficult part of leadership is not people management but managing our energy.

To be a natural leader and bring about massive changes in your results, you've got to keep the remote control of your energy with you. The problem is we have given remote control to everyone around us to make us feel happy or sad, successful or failed, victim or master. Everything and

HOW I'M DRAINING ME	HOW I'M RENEWING ME
PHYSICAL ENERGY:	PHYSICAL ENERGY:
EMOTIONAL ENERGY:	EMOTIONAL ENERGY:
MENTAL ENERGY:	MENTAL ENERGY:
SPIRITUAL ENERGY:	SPIRITUAL ENERGY:

FIGURE P2.1
Energy map.

anything at work disturbs us quickly, be it the results, people's behaviors, or circumstances. Within moments, our moods and feelings change. We may not realize how we allow people to control our actions, behaviors, and thoughts. Work on its own is never stressful. We cannot manage our energy, which causes stress. The problem to be solved in today's corporates and business world is becoming more innovative while maintaining a sense of control over the self.

Authentic leaders can invoke the power within them to decide how they feel and act every day, irrespective of people's behaviors and circumstances. You can create your own experiences and environment at your workplace.

Refuse to be dependent. Refuse to be a remote-controlled leader. External circumstances are never entirely in our control, but your inner situation is in your control. What is needed is a new way of thinking and responding to people and situations.

Remember, the more you transfer positive energy to your employees, the more job engagement you have and the more successful you will be.

LEADERSHIP CHALLENGE

Connect with everyone around you by radiating positive relational energy in different ways.

Power 3

Focus on Your Game

Someone approached me as I sat at the J.W. Marriott coffee shop in India, writing this chapter.

He tells me that he heard me when I came to do a session at his company for the senior leadership team and that he follows my leadership insights on my social media platforms. We clicked a few pictures and spoke for a couple of minutes.

Before I excused myself to complete this chapter, he asked me something that made me change the entire content of this chapter from what I had intended to write.

His question was, "Payal, how do you stay ahead of your competitors?"

Now, it's a question I've been personally asked numerous times, and I always have only one answer, "I don't have any competitors."

And please, I say this not out of pride or immodesty but in complete honesty.

I believe I am here to deliver what I am best at and serve the corporate world professionals. I am not here to compete but to deliver the best I can. I am here to share my work to help leaders grow and be successful.

And so, I don't look around at competitors and their actions.

I see many of us in the corporate world trying to compete with others, wasting our limited time, extensive talents, and a powerhouse of energy in blowing off someone else's candle rather than lighting up our spirits.

Knowing what's happening around you is good, but never be consumed by competing. Instead, learn from the best people around you, embrace those qualities, and up your game each day. Great leaders are constantly working on making themselves better each day.

Have you heard about Pablo Casas, one of the greatest cellist players ever lived? He started playing at 12 and accomplished things that no other musician had. He was known around the world as the best in his field. At 85, he still got up every morning and practiced 5 hours daily. A reporter asked him why he still put so much effort into it. He smiled and said, I think I'm getting better.

What are you getting better at each day?

Make yourself such in your industry that there never was anyone like you before you, and there will not be anyone like you after you.

As Howard Cosell puts it, "The ultimate victory in competition is derived from the inner satisfaction of knowing that you have done your best and have gotten the most out of what you had to give."

You are here in the corporate world to make a difference like no one else. If you are going to be worried about competing, then you have nothing left in you to up your game.

If you genuinely want to stay ahead, make it a habit of being a better version of yourself each day. Commit to giving your best, and you rate your best each day.

Reaching the top will require tremendous focus on running your race. Otherwise, you will be distracted by everyone and everything around you. You must have the ability to center your attention on your game.

You have to be intentional about your growth. You have to plan your development. Growth is not automatic. It's not accidental. What steps are you taking to make your growth intentional?

Allowing your mind to become fixed on worrying about people's opinions or negative past experiences can spiral into self-doubt. Focus is a fragile trait, so learning to stay mentally focused on your game is a much-needed skill for you to learn.

When you focus on your game, you push yourself harder when everyone else has had enough.

Most C.E.O.s I associate with never lost sight of where they were headed. They knew they wanted to become the C.E.O. and made conscious choices. They played their game and focused on their game.

Apostle Paul reminds us in 1 Cor. 3:9: "Do you not know that in a race, all the runners run their very best to win, but only one receives the prize? Run [your race] to seize the prize and make it yours!"

The universe has laid before you a different race, so it is essential to keep focused and be disciplined enough not to compare your distances and race to another person.

Most people are not enjoying their career life and aren't getting ahead because they have stepped out of their tracks and are trying to fit into someone else's shoes.

―――――――

STOP DISTRACTING YOURSELF FROM SUCCESS

Today, everyone is distracted. Everyone, from kids to adults, finds it hard to focus on their game. We get into what I call the shiny object syndrome. You will read all about it in Chapter 19.

Working to stay mentally focused requires understanding the significant distractions that present themselves during competition. In my two decades of work with leaders, I have noticed five major distractions that are most common and which do not allow us to reach the top.

Distraction # 1 – The People: The noise we hear and the things people tell us all consume us. As they say, a ship never sinks because of the water around it but because of the water that enters it. The people we are surrounded by significantly impact who we are and who we become, and as much as we think the ones around us won't affect us, they do.

Distraction # 2 – The Future: Because we don't know what will happen next, the burden of not knowing becomes an ever-present anxiety. We live in fear of the "other shoe" dropping, the notion that the very worst is yet to come. If our current crisis has revealed anything about us, it's our illusion that we can control everything.

Distraction # 3 – Your Own Mind: We lack mental focus and are drifting from thought to thought. One of the easiest mental rabbit trails we go down is wondering what might happen instead of paying attention to what is occurring. We begin to imagine scenarios that have little foundation in reality.

Distraction #4 – Your Environment: This is being preoccupied with everything that could go wrong. We begin to see the worst in every situation, choosing to focus on problems rather than opportunities. This thinking creeps into our relationships and disconnects us from others, which fuels further negative thinking.

Distraction #5 – The Information Overload: Too much information about an issue inhibits the ability to focus appropriately on the most significant concepts and messages. The constant influx of information can reduce dopamine levels, leading to a loss of motivation and focus. This can ultimately harm one's self-confidence, as users feel like they are not doing enough compared to others.

DISCOVER YOUR GREATNESS

Put some dried grass in the sun; nothing happens, even on the hottest day. Put the dried grass under a magnifying glass, and the grass catches on fire. The sun's focused rays are more powerful than they are without focus. The same is true for people who want to reach the top.

Michael Jordan, the best basketball player in history, did not negotiate his contracts, design his uniforms, and prepare his travel schedules. He focused his time and energies on what he did best: playing basketball.

The great jazz soloist Louis Armstrong did not spend time selling tickets to his shows or setting up chairs for the audience. He concentrated on his point of brilliance: playing the trumpet. The solution is to be ultra-focused on the main job.

As a newly promoted manager, Philips attended a conference on communication where the keynote speaker captured his heart, and she said, "I wish I were an orator like that." Later on, a successful entrepreneur caught his attention, and he stated, "I wish I were an entrepreneur too." But, down the line, he realized he had an unusual gift of influencing anyone who came across him. He went on to develop his talent and became one of the most successful C.E.O.s of all time.

I know of a fashion designer, Margaret, who achieved incredible success over the past thirty years, dressing the wealthy and celebrities. She also began her fashion stores; today, they have ten spread across America and Canada.

Recently, when I met her over golf, I asked Margaret to tell me the secret to her success.

And one thing she said struck a chord.

She told me a big part of her ability to break through in a highly competitive industry was that she followed her path, not being too influenced by others.

You may look at others and wish you had their talents, abilities, and opportunities. But search within yourself and discover the skills that are hidden in you. When your destiny revolves around your talents, you will shine brighter than ever.

There are several dimensions to focus on. You can specialize in your industry or company. You can be an expert in a limited set of functional skills. Or you can gain the highest knowledge in a particular domain of your field.

Focus turns out to be the least used leadership power most of the time. We get distracted by everything and by everyone, like this granddad and grandson who were on their way to town with a donkey. The granddad walked while the boy rode on the donkey. Somebody pointed and said, "Look at that selfish boy making the old man walk." Hearing that, the boy got down, and the granddad got onto the donkey and started riding. Soon, somebody else criticized the old man for making the little boy walk. So, both of them got onto the donkey and began riding. Soon, somebody else criticized them for being such a "heavy load" on the donkey. By the time they reached town, they were both carrying the donkey.

Here's my point: if you don't dig your heels in and stand up to pursue your dreams, you will be tossed to and from every idea and comment from people. Forget what people say and focus on your race.

I have seen that playing their own game is a common trait all successful people possess.

It's not that these people have succeeded because they've had it any easier than others – it's just that they've learned to focus on what they want to achieve.

How do you stay true to yourself and your instincts when so many people around you shout "NO?" Here's how they do it.

YOU'VE GOT TO A.D.D

One of the acronyms I teach leaders is called A.D.D.

1. **Avoid Comparing Yourself to Others**: My mom always says that each of us has been given a different question paper about life, so never compare your answers with someone else's. She couldn't have

been more correct on this. I see many people trying to emulate other leaders rather than developing their leadership style. You improve your speed by focusing on investing, creating, and growing your traits and abilities. Reaching the top requires you to boost your uniqueness.

2. **Define What "Success" Looks Like for You**: Your definition of success and my definition of success might be very different. If you aren't clear about what you want, you will be pulled in all directions. So take some time and be clear on what success means to you and how you would know you've achieved it, with a crystal clear sense of what the finish line looks like.

3. **Disrupt Old Thinking Patterns**: Great leaders who make it to the top are revolutionaries. They challenge conventional thinking and believe in doing things differently. Begin to look at the world through an inquisitive, investigative lens. Create new ways of doing things.

Following your path often means being prepared to give the status quo a bit of a rattle.

In a world full of perfectly curated lives displayed across various social media, the constant pressure to compare yourself to others can be overwhelming. It's easy to get wrapped up in what other people do and feel you must compete.

Just because someone else follows a particular path doesn't mean you have to do it. The universe has given you your path. Enrich and nourish your path.

I had learned from my father always to stand out and stand tall. Both my girls were born and raised in America, and this is one lesson I've passed to them, too: don't try to fit in, but learn to play your own game well. It is one of the hardest things in the world to do. But I can assure you, once you learn how to focus on your game, you will speed up your game like never before.

Like what my dear friend and the Chief Business Officer of a company, Atit Mehta always tell me, "focus on the input not on the output. The input is in your hands and do whatever you can at the input stage. The output will take care of itself."

LEADERSHIP CHALLENGE

Focus entirely on your game.

Power 4

Develop the Ability of Distanced Thinking

Imagine you are the senior vice president of finance in a Fortune 500 company. On a particular day, you and your two colleagues are in the boardroom to join a Zoom meeting with the C.E.O. of the company and a few external stakeholders for a critical discussion about a significant reorganization within the company and moving the operations from hardware to software. You are trying to share your perspective on how this could negatively impact the company's bottom line. The debate goes tangent and gets heated up. While you continue to put your point forward aggressively, the C.E.O. puts you on mute on the Zoom call, and you can no longer say anything while he takes over and continues the discussion.

What would you do if this happened to you?

Well, let me tell you what a friend, Rakesh, did in this case. He was furious, and the anger was evident on his face. He shut his laptop, stood up, looked at his two colleagues, and said, "I am done with this company." For the next few weeks, he felt awkward whenever Rakesh would be around this C.E.O. He behaved irrationally around him. He would often ignore his calls and try to stay distanced from him. The C.E.O. approached Rakesh quite a few times to help resolve the situation. But Rakesh was adamant. Within a few weeks, Rakesh submitted his resignation and joined another company.

What concerns me about Rakesh even today is that he has moved into a new company, but it's the same old him with the same old thinking pattern. It's a matter of time before a similar incident repeats in his life, or a more significant incident might occur. Rakesh will behave like he did in his previous company, leading him to search for another company.

DOI: 10.4324/9781003439134-11

Many leaders face issues like Rakesh, where they cannot rise above a ten-feet view; they behave as if the crises were their devil. And so they make irrational decisions that haunt them later.

When experiencing negative emotions, we tend to go into 'first-person mode"—that is, our perspective is narrowed and limited to what we feel and see from our standpoint. We are zoomed in too much on the situation. As it's said, you cannot solve a problem with the same thinking with which you entered into it.

Your brain has a built-in ability to leverage an optical power that allows you to "distance out" and imagine seeing a situation as if you were viewing a stranger engaging in the event.

Distant thinking is an absolute internal leadership power you can harness when you consciously step back from a situation. This power alone can have a significant impact on your day-to-day life.

You can step back and observe yourself and your inner dialogue from afar. Why did I bring up the word inner dialogue? When a situation happens, we begin to zoom in close on it, which inflames our emotions to the exclusion of all the alternative ways of thinking. That's when a lot of mental chatter begins within us. We get drowned in self-doubt, anger, tension, and self-criticism and make decisions that do not allow us to reach where we want.

To gain more control over our internal dialogue, making it work for us rather than being a slave to it, successful leaders practice the distanced thinking technique – scientifically proven to channelize our mental chatter correctly.

Distant thinking is the process of stepping back and observing the situation from afar, which in turn will bring about a change in our inner dialogue.

When you are completely zoomed in, your mental chatter races negatively. Within 17 seconds, if you cannot break this chatter, your brain gets into a snowball effect, creating a massive ball of negativity.

Now let me warn you: often, our mental chatter is very positive, which creates the same snowball effect, where you make impulsive decisions.

You shouldn't make any decisions whenever you're sad, angry, upset, or even super happy. Just distancing yourself, waiting for a few days, or giving it a night to sleep on the decision will prevent you from making impulsive decisions that you might regret later.

DISTANCED THINKING TAKES EFFORT

Over the decades I have worked in the coaching industry, I've learned one big lesson about coaching people and life.

Nothing is simply good or bad.

It is either better or worse than the alternatives it is compared to. What works is the distanced thinking approach.

Your brain can see yourself from afar, as if you are in a helicopter, watching the situation from 30,000 feet above, getting complete coverage of the problem as a third party.

The one who reaches the top is not necessarily the fastest climber. The winner of the race is a quick climber who can also keep themselves on track, maintain their energy levels throughout the months, look at and understand the weather, make decisions, and repair themselves. It's a whole range of skills. Leaders have to master the art of zooming in and zooming out at the right times.

Distanced thinking is a simple five-step process.

1. *Zoom out without an immediate response when an unwanted incident occurs.*
2. *Survey the environment or the person.*
3. *Reflect on the course of action.*
4. *Observe yourself from afar in that action.*
5. *Decide if the action is beneficial.*

When you are distancing yourself from a situation, *you automatically increase* the distance from your egocentric perspective.

IT'S ALL ABOUT ADJUSTING YOUR FOCUS

As a regional manager in my early days at a company, I stood near the vending machine. I overheard one of my subordinates tell my peer I was not very supportive and that she mainly did not like working with me. Now, because two vending machines in our office cafeteria face each other, they could not see me and did not know I heard them. I immediately interrupted their conversation and told my subordinate I did not expect this from her and felt offended.

I refused to speak to her for the next few days, and my attitude toward her changed. I made it a point not to include her in some of my team meetings. I avoided my one-on-one meetings with her. I ignored her and rated her low on her performance. I even excluded her from big strategy decisions.

Looking back at this incident, I regret my behavior toward her. If I had practiced distanced thinking, zoomed out, and asked myself, "What is the best way through this?" my behavior would have been better toward this incident.

How often have we made an emotional decision, regretting it later? Many of us have been in a situation when our emotions prevent us from seeing the big picture and responding appropriately;

The lens through which leaders view the world can help or hinder their ability to make sound strategic decisions, especially during crises.

Great leaders constantly adjust their focus. They must continuously consider both the big picture and the details.

I have been quite fascinated with one of the industrialists I met at a client's annual event in London. At a very young age, he had achieved success, which many of us might see later in life. At the dinner table, I learned he is most well-known for his problem-solving ability. I asked him how he had mastered this ability. Here's what he said to me, "Payal, sometimes when trying to solve a problem, you're just unable to converge on an appropriate solution. You've tested everything – done all the permutations and combinations – but nothing helps. The problem cannot be solved."

In such situations, I decided to step away and gain perspective. I either take a break and return to the problem later with fresh eyes or create space by explaining the project to someone else. This way, I can reframe the situation and solve the problem like no one else.

When I coach executives on their ability to practice distanced thinking, it's hard to think objectively about something emotionally intense. Sitting with me, talking about it in session, they can often experience some distance from these emotions and observe the process as if they were on the bank of the imaginary river, watching themselves go down the rapids.

During the coaching sessions, one of my clients would complain about his team not listening to his instructions. He would continuously ask me, "Payal, what's wrong with them?' When he understood the power of distanced thinking, his question changed to "What can I do better in my communication so they can comprehend my instructions?"

In yet another case, one of the executives would often have problems with his teams and wonder why he always gets to work with incompetent people. When he practiced distanced thinking, his question changed to "What strengths do each of these people bring?"

This simple shift can be a game-changer in your professional relationships, teamwork, and leadership.

Distance thinking can be practiced by asking yourself simple questions such as: *Why am I getting so emotional about this? Why am I taking out my anger on this person? Does the way I'm acting help me be a better leader? Do I have the power not to act this way?*

These questions will lead you to a better awareness of what has brought you to this point and what you can do to improve your lives.

LEADERSHIP CHALLENGE

Zoom out of an unwanted situation and take a look from the outside before making a decision. See if it changed your actions and results.

Power 5

Work Like an Immigrant

"Work like an immigrant" is one lesson I have grown up with and passed on to my two girls. America is a nation of immigrants. And whether our forefathers were strangers who crossed the Atlantic, the Pacific, or the Rio Grande, we are here only because this country welcomed them in.

Twenty-five years in America, I must say, I've seen it all, with people born in the United States complaining about money, jobs, minimum wage, and how hard it is to live paycheck to paycheck. They grumble about our government. They whine about the police. And the list goes on.

Do you know who doesn't complain? Immigrants. Immigrants who've been given a chance to make something of their lives here. The life of an immigrant is tough.

They start as strangers having different cultural practices and unique ways of behaving. Some locals may look down on them and even make fun of them. It is not uncommon for immigrants to feel inadequate, unwelcome, or even suffer from low self-esteem. Yet, many have turned around their lives and achieved the impossible.

Many of my immigrant friends and business associates are happy to be here. They come here and make something of their lives.

I do consider myself fortunate to be in the United States. And I don't take my opportunity for granted. As an immigrant to the United States, I have learned so much from immigrants' life lessons that they have become part of my life.

In my previous neighborhood, one of my neighbors had come from the Philippines. The family of four included the dad, the mom, and two boys, ages eight and eleven.

As immigrants who came to this country, the father and mother worked in I.T. full-time jobs and raised the two kids.

 DOI: 10.4324/9781003439134-12

The dad also did several "side hustles." I have also observed how my neighbors went to work on days like Thanksgiving and Christmas while others took a holiday. They would rarely take off from work. They enjoyed their work though. At an early age, their children understood the value of work, and I often saw them helping their dad in the car wash or with groceries.

To succeed at work, I learned early on to work like an immigrant. Most of the top C.E.O.s and entrepreneurs here in America are immigrants. Google co-founder Sergey Brin was born in Communist Russia. The man who could take us to Mars, Elon Musk, is from South Africa. Arianna Huffington is the founder of the eponymous news site from Greece. And the list goes on.

I know Antonio, the founder of a great start-up in Silicon Valley whose family relocated to the United States from the Cibao region of the Dominican Republic. He comes from a humble family and with no silver spoon in his mouth. So, when he was 17, he started mowing lawns. Then, he learned to do snow removal. He then got a job waiting tables at restaurants while completing his undergrad. Then he'd go home, change clothes, and rush to the gas station nearby to work at the cash counter. At night, he showers and changes. The next day, he'd do it all over again.

We all need to have this work mentality like Antonio. I call it the "immigrant mentality."

YOU HAVE TO BE DETERMINED TO WIN

Immigrants wake up every day with joy just for the opportunity to go to work. Think about that. Their internal gratitude is about the chance to work.

Immigrants aren't sitting around complaining about their bosses. Or how long they had to work. Or how the economy of America is.

An immigrant mentality is a state of mind filled with gratitude, hardwork, and a "do whatever it takes" attitude. Their survival and planning skills are fantastic.

If you genuinely want to reach the top, embrace the immigrant men tality. A person with an immigrant mentality believes in always working hard for what they like. And that mentality never really goes away – it becomes your competitive advantage. You're not intimidated by pressure; you thrive on it.

Rohit was born in Chandigarh, India, where he completed his schooling and later his Business Administration in Marketing. He enrolled for further studies in the United States due to his academic excellence. While here, to sustain himself financially, he juggled between three odd jobs till he found a way to get out of that circle and enter the entrepreneurial world.

Rohit faced numerous challenges during his journey, as he had limited resources and a lack of business experience, which resulted in a few failed ventures. Despite all this, he did not give up. He believed in himself and strived to be the best he could be. Within seven years, he built his business empire.

Raina climbed the corporate ladder pretty soon in her career. Going from being an individual contributor to becoming the company's chief information officer in only 11 years was nothing short of a miraculous journey. She attributes her success to working harder than anyone else around her.

Raina would often volunteer to tackle new projects that excited her. She would work on improving processes in her current job. On weekends, she would invest time in her self-development. She was never tired of doing more. She would find opportunities to do more.

Great leaders believe in figuring things out and adapting to any environment. Being unafraid of new challenges and proactively reaching for them is extremely important for long-term business survival. They have a thirst for opportunity. As simple as it sounds, many times, the only thing that separates those at the mid-level from those at the top is pure determination. It's the thought process that makes a huge difference.

I have coached people from all fields of work. I have often observed that those who get stuck in their career are the ones who question themselves, asking, "Is the effort worth the reward to reach the top?" Meanwhile, those who reach the top are the ones who tell themselves, "I will do whatever it takes to get there."

Each day you wake up, ask yourself how determined you are to accomplish your P.A.S.

One of the things I have learned from immigrants is their quality to find solutions to everything. In 2014, when I came to India for corporate coaching, I learned a famously known word here – "jugaad." In the Western world, it is called "hacks."

Jugaad is your ability to make something out of nothing. To get the best from what you have without damaging anything or anyone. Now, immigrants come to the United States with less resources. So, they develop this art of making the most out of what they have.

Each day you wake up, ask yourself how determined you are to accomplish your P.A.S.

Making it to the top requires working with an immigrant mindset.

Table 5.1 shows the difference between leaders with a traditional mindset and those with an immigrant mindset. I encourage you to look at the table and identify which mindset you generally work with (Table P5.1).

One of the greatest discoveries I've made in the last two decades as a leadership coach is the realization that world-class leaders are driven by positive expectations. And immigrants work exactly with this mentality. They always expect to win and move ahead regardless of what they are up against. And they do this by visualizing growth and a great life for themselves and their children. And in most cases, it works in their favor. Why? Because it creates a never-give-up attitude in them. They understand the stress and struggle it will take for them to be successful in an unknown country. If each of us works with an immigrant mindset, we will become mentally tough, pushing ourselves to win over every challenge at our workplace.

TABLE P5.1

Difference between Leaders with a Traditional Mindset and Those with an Immigrant Mindset

Traditional Mindset	Immigrant Mindset
Complaining	Gratitude
Limited in their way of thinking	Figure it out
Give up	Survive, thrive, and win
Complains about long work hours	Believes in always working hard
Settle with what they could achieve	Pushed through unimaginable hardships
Weak-willed	Persistent and determined
Focuses on work–life balance	No work–life balance, only integration
Works on intermittent fusillades	**Generate continuous momentum with small steps**
Thinks of excuses	Thinks only of ways to succeed
Take what comes and work on it	Wired for opportunities
Intimidated by pressure	Thrives in pressure

Most people who have reached the top have worked with an immigrant mentality. Those who want to get to the top must work harder than anyone else. It's challenging but doable.

Making it to the top means working hard and testing your limits to get results. Giving your best to your company encourages your employees to do the same.

My father would always say that you should work harder than everyone else around you. Work so hard on the work you have that the work feels no one can do it better than you.

Now I realize that even if you could work 24 hours daily, there is only so much time to accomplish the needed tasks on your to-do list. So what's the solution? Instead of fitting more into your calendar, experiment with ways to get more out of the same amount of time. Essentially, the key to exponential success is to work smarter and more complex.

Successful people in every field are often said to be "blessed with talent" or even just lucky. But the truth is, many worked harder than the average person can even imagine.

Here is something I want you to remember. Too many leaders have become accustomed to giving their best at their job. To make it to the top, you've got to go beyond your best.

LEADERSHIP CHALLENGE

Start developing an immigrant mindset by picking one mindset at a time and working on it.

Power 6

Be Unpredictable

It's a lovely sunny morning, and the manufacturing firm's employees in Baltimore relax, sipping coffee and chatting in the office cafeteria. The clock strikes eight, and everyone is back at their workstation. When Clair, the company's managing director, enters the office at 8.00 am, she is happy to see her people engrossed in work. At around 7.00 pm, when Clair leaves the office for home, she feels proud seeing most employees at their desks still working. She feels her team is super dedicated. However, on the day of her performance review with her boss, she was surprised that she was told that her team was not performing well.

What's wrong?

The problem is that the employees were working just for show. They knew their boss Clair would arrive at the top at 8.00 am. Most of them hung around in the evening until 7.00 because they knew Clair leaves by 7.00 pm, too.

Many of us, like Clair, fix our days and work time. In the era of hybrid work, our employees know which days we would be coming to work and what time we would leave. Many leaders have taken advantage of the hybrid work model and have kept a routine schedule.

When your people know your schedule and how you act or respond, they behave in a particular way to impress you. When I ask leaders what their work schedule is like, I often hear this phrase: "As long as you get your three days in office, it's all set." And so, to some extent, they've fixed their three days of work from the office.

The best leaders always have a flexible work schedule. They keep an erratic one.

Most of us are predictable leaders. The monthly C.E.O. brief, the quarterly management briefing, and the end-of-year thank-you message to all staff. The same way of conducting your one-on-one meetings. It's no wonder employees have tuned out. Robust and stable leadership is essential. However, equally important in today's world is dynamic, vibrant leadership.

Throughout my career, I have noticed that only a few predictable employees found their way up the career ladder.

Predictable leaders seldom reach the top because they never break the rules. They don't challenge the status quo. They get into high comfort levels.

Learning to be unpredictable can help you gain power by taking your competitors by surprise. Remember this: people generally crave predictability because it gives them control. When you become even slightly unpredictable, you can throw others off balance.

I once met the managing director of a steel manufacturing company who told me he comes to the office on days he has no meetings. He prefers to take virtual meetings from home and be at the office without virtual meetings. This way, he can spend time with his people when he is at work, and his people have no idea of the days he would come to work.

Keeping your work schedule a mystery can give you a competitive advantage in today's hot and competitive market. When you suddenly arrive early for a meeting or at the office, you get extra information you'd miss otherwise. When you're early, you can talk with influential people already there.

Many leaders are predictable because you must put in the extra effort to be unpredictable. For instance, creating a flexible schedule will demand more work from you. It will mean you will not be committed to a three-day work-from-home schedule at the office and to a two-day schedule. You cannot fix which days you will be going to work. And it is surely going to disrupt your work and home balance. It could mean there are weeks when you are landing up all five days at work. Are you prepared for this? Because reaching the top demands you to break your routine and get out of your comfort life.

And don't get me wrong. It's not about micromanagement. It is not about creating fear. Undoubtedly, an unpredictable leadership style has often been associated with leaders creating fear in their people. But think about it; some fear is always reasonable. Your employees will try to give their best because they are still determining how you will respond or when you will show up.

Unpredictability is an essential tool for wielding power. Suddenly doing something no one expected creates some healthy fear and confusion.

Robert joined a technology startup in London, leading product management for its toolbar. From his early days at the company, Robert would reach the office by 7.00 am (an hour earlier than the rest of the people working there). He would often take that time to read his emails and prepare for upcoming meetings. During this time, Robert walked around the quiet, empty office.

A couple of times he came across Charles, the head of the coding department, who also happened to reach the office around seven thirty in the morning. They would often have quick conversations in the hallway. One day, Charles happened to talk to Robert about a weakness he had identified in the company's software strategy; Robert researched this and got some valuable and critical data for Charles, which helped him. Soon, they both worked on some vital projects together. Charles saw clear evidence of Robert's strategic thinking and ability to challenge the status quo.

Soon, Robert ascended from director of product management to vice president of product management to product chief while managing some of the company's highest-profile and strategically essential products.

No doubt he worked hard and had good strategic thinking ability. But one thing I know Robert continues to do is have a mysterious schedule. No one around him knows when he will show up or retire for the day.

Once these leaders set a routine, they break it and create a new one. That is why you find them and their schedule mysterious.

If the best in the world are stretching themselves to give their best, why aren't you?

Start your morning with something different; look to break the routine where possible. Share job responsibilities between team members and look to introduce new roles where possible. Giving your team a chance to take on new challenges, learn new skills, and fill their knowledge gaps will help keep them engaged and productive. Make an effort to break up the routine across the office. Change up when and where regular meetings take place.

RAISE YOUR INTERNAL STANDARDS

Why would you want to be unpredictable?

Because while your competitors, inside and outside of the organization, are stressing themselves out, trying their best to anticipate what you're doing, you can achieve your objectives almost unnoticed. Sometimes, you must learn to be unpredictable to gain power over a situation.

You can use this tactic effectively even if you are the underdog. For instance, during the Civil War, General Stonewall Jackson confused and stymied the much larger Union forces marching on Richmond by repeatedly moving north and back south. In response, Union General George McClellan slowed his troops while trying to figure out what was happening, giving the South time to reinforce Richmond. This turned an inevitable defeat into a draw. General Jackson knew how to be unpredictable, which worked to his advantage.

Learn from Bobby Fischer on how to be unpredictable. In 1972, chess great Bobby Fischer so unnerved Russian champion Boris Spassky unpredictably that Spassky had a meltdown and left without completing the match in Reykjavik, Iceland.

Fischer defeated Spassky by keeping him in a state of confusion. This is an excellent example of how to be unpredictable.

During a coaching session with Serra, a company's senior vice president, she told me how frustrated she was in dealing with one of her peer executives. This peer of hers would talk significantly less during their one-to-one meetings and refrain from sharing information. He would test her patience on many aspects of the work. He often needed more time to complete his side of the work on a project, and eventually, Serra would extend the deadline for him or get it done.

I helped Serra understand her predictable qualities like empathy, collaboration, and calmness. But, I also encouraged her to be unpredictable in her responses and actions. Her peer had understood that if he talked less, Serra would eventually try to be emphatic and speak up more, thereby sharing more information with him than needed. I asked Serra to lose her cool at times and show some tantrums. And at times, to remain calm in a similar situation and show empathy. I suggested she be unpredictable, which helped Serra deal well with her peer executive and get him to complete the work strategically.

Sometimes, the problem isn't in what we want but in the "how" we're trying to make it happen.

Getting into the habit of being unpredictable requires you to raise your internal standards.

The process of being unpredictable requires inner work. It is not enough to read; you must practice what you read, which needs time and effort.

TURN THE TABLES

In the corporate world, beginners are not unpredictable. Experts are much more. Now, here's a word of caution. Too much unpredictability will be seen as a sign of indecisiveness. Such power should only be used judiciously.

To reiterate, this cannot only be used to "terrify," but it can be used for positive things like creating energy, excitement, and passion by doing something you've never done before.

To become unpredictable, you must first answer these questions: "What makes me predictable?" "It's your habits, right?"

Habits make you a "Routine" type of person; even good habits. So, if you want to be unpredictable, then break the habits. It's healthy to break it from time to time or change its pattern.

That's the start. Breaking habits will open a new path in your mind, that you are not conditioned with some daily customized actions.

Be unpredictable in your behavior, in your thinking, in your schedule, and in your response.

Turn the tables. Be deliberately unpredictable. As a leader, your people are always trying to read the motives behind your actions and to use your predictability against you. Throw in an inexplicable move, and you put them on the defensive.

Let's say you've maintained a habit within your team where you have habituated yourselves to doing the same thing every week—you've become predictable.

By "throwing in a completely inexplicable move," you can create spontaneity, excitement, and passion by stepping away from the same old habit and doing something you've never done before.

Now, here's a word of caution. Too much unpredictability will be seen as a sign of indecisiveness. Be selective about when and how you use unpredictability. Don't be unpredictable all the time. If you're too unpredictable, people will start to see you as unreliable or untrustworthy. This power should only be used judiciously.

Being unpredictable does not mean it is used to "terrify." Still, it can be used for positive things like creating energy, excitement, and passion by doing something you've never done before.

Someone once said that the definition of insanity is doing the same thing repeatedly and expecting a different result. Making even tiny, seemingly irrelevant changes to your daily patterns – taking a different route to work or rearranging furniture – can stimulate nerve cells and boost the production of neurotrophins, which help brain cells thrive: the less routine, the more life.

In 1974, Muhammad Ali did this with George Foreman. Ali had a particular style of fighting that everyone knew him for. He moved and danced around a lot, using his quickness to get the better of his opponent. Many were tipping Foreman to win because of his massive power. Ali realized he needed to change his style of fight to have a chance at winning. Sometimes, before fights, trainers would loosen the ropes around the ring if the boxers intended to "slug it out."

Ali's trainer did this before the fight, yet no one believed those were his real intentions. People assumed it was a trick. To the world's shock, he changed his habit of 10 years of fighting. He went up against the ropes and slugged it out, upsetting Foreman's strategy. Foreman wore himself out by throwing punches wildly as Ali eventually knocked him out.

Being unpredictable is a powerful tool that can increase your power, make you more interesting, and achieve your goals.

Psychologists have discovered that humans crave novelty and change. Yet most of us stay in the safe harbor of the known. We think we'll be happier and more secure in the familiar world of the known.

Learning to be unpredictable can help you gain power by taking your competitors and team by surprise. Learn to be formless—that is, flexible, fluid, and unpredictable—and your opponents won't be able to get a handle on you. *Don't be locked into a single system, process, strategy, or approach. Change to suit your needs and circumstances.*

To stand out, you must do things differently without losing uniqueness. Deciding to do things differently can lead to new experiences, opportunities, and perspectives. Unpredictability inserts spontaneity into your lifestyle. It pushes you to try new things, meet new people, visit new places, and broaden your perspectives. Regularly stepping outside your comfort zone keeps life fresh and vibrant, and facing your fears and embracing the unknown leads to tremendous growth.

LEADERSHIP CHALLENGE

Take some time to think about your business or your career. Are there any areas where you've become a little complacent? *Now, challenge your old ways of being, thinking, and doing to make room for the new. See in what ways you can be unpredictable.*

Power 7

Bet on Yourself

I'm in the office of Mr Lucas, the C.E.O. of a financial company in the heart of Manhattan. I arrived almost thirty minutes early, which I do on purpose to observe in real time how they think and behave while at work. While I get seated in his office, I see him hurriedly clearing a backlog of voicemails, trying to get to them before our meeting starts.

While he goes through all his messages, half of which are sales pitches, which he deletes even before they start, I gaze out of the window of his office on the 27th floor of the tall glass building. Outside the window, the view is fantastic. You can see the vast green park with people walking, jogging, sitting under the tree, and some people walking their dogs.

As I admired the view, I saw Lucas interestingly hear a message: "Hi Lucas, this is Sheela. Marc suggested I contact you?" Lucas spoke his mind aloud, looking at me and saying, "Hmmm ... I wonder who Sheela is? I've never heard this name before. But it does not look like a sales call because I know Marc, and he wouldn't refer anyone to me for sales." So Lucas immediately calls Marc and gets to know that Marc referred Lucas for a board of director position in a company where Sheela is currently the C.E.O. I see Lucas happy, and he connects with Sheela. Their conversation is brief, and Lucas gets all the necessary information within ten minutes. As he hangs up the phone, I ask, "So, you seem happy about this. Is this something in your line of work?" Lucas can't shake the smile off his face when he says, "No, it's in the IT industry, and I've never worked in any IT firm. But, yes, it's interesting, and I will take it up. I kind of love figuring things out in uncharted territories. It's brought me to where I am. We'll see what happens."

Lucas was right. Coaching Lucas for the past nine months, I knew this trait of his is exactly what brought him here.

     DOI: 10.4324/9781003439134-14

For many of us, a proposition in an entirely unknown industry would create doubts. We would hesitate to enter into the unknown. We would plan our journey meticulously and not deviate from our plan. We prefer to stay in our lane and not try anything in an unknown territory.

Unapologetically ambitious people are open to taking risks and experimenting with their career life. Those who have reached the top have confidently stepped into the unknown. They bet on themselves each day.

Betting on yourself means – a commitment to your future, a willingness to pursue what you love, an unyielding belief in your abilities, and the discipline to stay focused and follow through. Your ability to bet on yourself will determine between a life of mediocrity and one of extraordinary potential.

What Lucas said about "figuring things out in uncharted territories" and "we'll see what happens" are typical thinking patterns of successful people. Success begins with figuring things out, making choices, planning, and seeing where your preferences take you. All of these become a strong safety net that builds confidence and allows these leaders to enter the unknown.

And I must admit, for many years in my career, I've been extremely cautious and unable to step into the unknown. My parents and my schooling never taught me to take risks. I was raised in an environment of protection where every step was taken cautiously. I must say, it never helped in the long run.

Now let me warn you here. These super-successful leaders who make it to the top are not reckless in their decisions. They don't just impulsively jump into unknown territories. At the same time, their decision to enter the unknown is not out of fear.

Have you been afraid to step out and do something new because you don't know how it will work out? For most of us, fear grips us and alters our thinking; because of this, we are afraid to enter uncharted territories. The fear of the unknown is more significant than the unknown itself.

Don't let the "what ifs" talk you out of it. "What if I fail? What if they say no? What if I don't have the funds?" You'll never know unless you try. Think about this: When you come to the end of your career, will you have more regrets from the risks that you took or from the risks you didn't take?

I have had some amazing C.E.O.s on my leadership podcast. And if you were to listen to them, you would know how they all have dared to step into the unknown. They are great planners, and at the same time, they are risk-takers.

They love to experiment. And by no way do I want you to feel that their experiments have always been successful. Most of them have faced disappointments and setbacks. They learned from them, and every experiment they failed helped them make better decisions to a point where they succeeded to great heights. But, these setbacks never deterred their will to keep stepping into the unknown.

The play-it-safe paradox works well if you want to remain average. There is a reason why the majority of us are afraid of treading the waters in uncharted oceans of our career life. Let me ask you something, "What are our brains designed for?" Some say our brains are designed for success. That is why you hear motivational speakers telling you constantly that you are made to succeed.

Well, not really. If you look at the evolution of humanity, you will understand that our brains are designed for survival. The first thing when layoffs are announced in the company, what are you thinking about? You are thinking about survival – hoping your name isn't on that list. You are not thinking about your goals and what you want to achieve; you are only concerned about survival during the layoff period. And so, because we are wired for survival, we've grown up hearing words and phrases like "no," "stay away," "be very careful," "stay away from," "better safe than sorry," etc. All messages are designed to keep us secure.

We were always taught to live cautiously by our well-wishers and society. And so we are afraid of treading the waters in uncharted oceans of our career life.

There comes a time in everyone's lives when these motivational messages no longer help. The same messages that were designed to help us become successful, in reality, block our growth. We are being overly cautious in our career moves, too.

Recently, in a media interview for the Atlanta Business Channel, I was asked, "Payal, how do you stay on top of your game?" And my answer was that the game never stays the same – and nor do I.

Every morning, you've got to wake up with a healthy fear that the business environment is changing and a conviction that, to win, you have to change faster and be more agile than anyone else.

For every leader I've coached, I tell them that the only way to discover their potential is to try new things constantly. As Nicola Yoon said, "Not doing anything is a risk. It's up to you."

I know many leaders I coach who want to innovate and create something different. But in their day-to-day work life, they are not willing to experiment.

Many of us are capable of outstanding performance, but we are afraid to take chances. Think of the last time someone approached you with a new idea, or you had a great idea that you were quick to dismiss. Most new ideas never surpass our ego, fear, and disbelief.

We are all dying of mental stagnation, and our minds are no longer fertile with new ideas.

FIGURE IT OUT

I was once given a precious word of wisdom by the chairman of a company, which I always cherish and practice. He told me, "Payal, once you are in the corporate world, learn these three words and apply them, and those words are: 'figure it out.'" Since then, I've been able to experiment and try new things in my career. That's how I gained the courage to leave corporate America and enter the coaching business's unknown territory. With every small risk I took, I got bolder to take that leap from America to India to help companies and leaders here with their executive coaching needs. Today, I have numerous companies in India too who hire me for my coaching and workshops.

What separates average leaders from world-class leaders? In my work with some of the top leaders, I can assure you none of them is cut from a different cloth than any of us. What makes them distinct is their ability to enter into the unknown constantly. And you can do it, too. Embrace option thinking, where you ask new questions to get new answers. Get a fresh perspective by putting yourself in a new environment. The best leaders see risk-taking and experimentation as a series of small steps – measured, thoughtful, and intentional.

The poet Constantine Cavafy penned the classic work "Ithaka," which illuminates all that's available to you when you intentionally take risks each day. The poem encourages you to set out for Ithaka on a road that is long, full of adventure, and full of discovery.

In today's generation, we are all comfortable with the navigation system that gives you the "Route overview," telling you about every turn coming up, where to expect traffic, and your estimated arrival time. And so, with the navigation system in our hands, we are confident to drive onto new roads.

Wouldn't it be great if you had a living system like this for your career? That would tell you where the money was coming from, how long it would take to reach your goal, and which right people would be there. If we had all the details, stepping into the unknown would be easy. But God doesn't give us details. He's not going to show you a blueprint for your whole life. And so, few successful people have trained their brains to build on faith rather than fear. Their faith isn't blinded. It's well structured and analyzed, which gives them the boldness to step into the unknown, where doors will open that you could have never opened, the right people will show up, and you'll have the funds and resources you need.

The scripture says, "God's word is a lamp unto our feet and a light unto our path." Personally, this testament helped me decide to step out of America and come to India to set up my leadership coaching work here. This statement means that you will never be able to see the complete picture. Just as the car headlights switched on at night can help you see only a hundred feet ahead of you. And if you keep driving as you go further, you will see more.

Similarly, you have the lamp of faith, knowledge, experience, talent, and ability. Use this light to see what's a hundred feet ahead of you. Don't stop yourself because you can't see the final destination. You never will see the final destination. And even if you took the risk and things went south, remember, you are alive and have the lamp with you to move ahead. Your faith is your biggest navigation system, and leaders at the top know how to use it. That's how they bet on themselves.

YOUR BIG LIFE DESIGN

If you're going to step into the unknown, there's going to be tension, anxiety, and nervousness. It's not always going to make sense. People may not understand it. Your thoughts will tell you, "You better play it safe. This is too big a risk. What if it doesn't work out? What if you don't have a supportive boss for the next project?"

If you take the first step, not knowing all the details but keeping your lamp with you, I assure you, you will learn how to bet on yourself and step into the unknown. That's where success awaits you.

You did not join the workforce, dependent on your boss or external circumstances. Your boss and circumstances will change, but your light will be with you and grow with you. Depends more on your lamp than on anything else.

Don't let the what-ifs talk you out of it. "What if I fail? What if they say no? What if I don't have the funds?" You'll never know unless you try. And when you come to the end of life, will you have more regrets about the risks you took or those you didn't take?

I studied the life of Fredrick Douglass, who said that we don't get everything we fight for, but everything we get will be a fight.

Every day, we face challenges, fears, obstacles, and negativity that hit us with left jabs and right hooks. We get so caught up in the details of bills, job pressures, raising kids, fixing the house, car payments, trying to make a living, and a hundred other to-dos that we can't even see our future success.

There is greatness in you. There is a Big Life plan for you. A smooth sea never made a skilled surfer, and a struggle-free existence never made a meaningful, extraordinary life.

THE GIFT OF IMPERFECTION

Many of us believe that to bet on ourselves, we must be perfect. There is beauty in imperfection, too. It's hard to look at what you might see as your weaknesses or faults. Yet, they are not faults or failures but rather pathways toward self-discovery and growth.

In Japan, there's an ancient custom called *Kintsugi*, meaning "to repair something with gold," where broken pottery is repaired with liquid gold or lacquer dusted with gold, which seals all the broken pieces of pottery not only together but also dramatically results in a unique piece of art, which is much more beautiful than the original.

If you've ever heard about *wabi-sabi*, you'd know what I'm talking about. The concept of wabi-sabi lingers around the idea that there's a kind of beauty in imperfection. Kintsugi is based on it strictly, which celebrates the beauty of broken and damaged things much more than the original pieces.

Back in the 15th century, this guy named *Ashikaga Yoshimasa* had accidentally broken his favorite tea cup, and guess where he sent it for repair? China!

When it returned from China, it didn't look the same anymore; it was mended with unpleasant metal staples. Ashikaga Yoshimasa became very disappointed and sad when he saw how ugly his teacup became. Then, he ordered his artisans to look for more flattering means of repair. So, the potters decided to fill the cracks with the lacquered resin and powdered gold. And what happened next is history. The broken ceramic had become a work of art.

So, he turned something broken and ugly into something beautiful!

From then on, the Japanese would sometimes break perfect ceramics to have them mended in gold. And these damaged pots fetched a higher price than their flawless counterparts.

Kintsugi is a difficult concept to be absorbed by people sometimes, but it does make sense.

All your heartbreaks transform you into something new and beautiful, just as the old cliché goes: *that which does not kill us makes us stronger.*

We all come with past baggage, with unseen scars. But the sooner we accept our breaks and cracks and fill them with gold, the sooner we will transform into something even more worthwhile to this entire existence. Do not try to hide them or act like these scars don't exist; it's perfectly normal; we all have them. It's about time to proudly wear your gold-filled scars, cracks, and crevices as badges and medals.

None of us is perfect. In many ways, we are all broken and damaged. And that's where your strength lies. Bet on yourself even when you are down and broken from within because you will come out better than your original self. Each time you embrace your imperfections, you will receive a dose of personal strength and conviction for how awesome you are.

Remember this, my friend, the biggest bet you can ever make is the bet on yourself. You are replaceable to your employer. The question is not if, but when your employer decides on your future, what is your plan? Are you going to become a helpless victim of external circumstances? Or will you have prepared yourself for a life where you have the power to decide your future? And the longer you wait to take risks, the less of a choice it becomes.

To get to world-class, becoming a spectacularly good innovator is essential. You've got to figure out how to make things better and discover new ways to add value, work smarter, and move faster – there are core creative traits that the best in business live by. It's always one small step after another.

Those who bet on themselves will surely reach the top because they are committed to getting there. Place any obstacles in their way, and they will take them as stepping stones to climb higher. When you bet on yourself, you decide to do whatever it takes to succeed.

You've got so much more to discover about what you can do. And you can only find your potential when you begin stepping into the unknown.

Trust that a plan is designed for you, and let the possibilities unfold. You will discover the great things you were born to do in the process. You don't have to push. Trust and your destiny will meet you when the time is right.

LEADERSHIP CHALLENGE

What unknown territory could you enter into that will take your career upward? Move ahead with your lamp of faith, knowledge, experience, talent, and ability into a new unknown territory.

Power 8

Attract Your Sponsors

Have you ever wondered why some people appear luckier than others? Like that young lady in your office who was quickly promoted ahead of you? Or that man who got a double salary increment over you? I've asked myself if they are more intelligent and hardworking.

Then, one day, a very close business associate and my mentor, the chairman of the Reggio-based preschools in India, told me something I would never forget. I now teach it to my clients, too. He said, "Payal, always know that decisions about you, your promotion, your salary hike, your projects, everything is made behind closed doors when you aren't around. So make sure people speak up for you and amplify your work best."

This lesson has helped me tremendously, not only while in corporate America but even after stepping out and establishing any coaching business.

Many people in the corporate world believe they will get to the top if they work hard and well.

Take, for instance, my client Geeta, an associate attorney in a well-known law firm in Delhi, India. Geeta is fabulous at her job. She meets with her clients to assess their needs. She conducts research using legislation, case law, and other legal texts as sources to decide on a modus operandi. She represents clients well at meetings, hearings, and trials. She can present her case and argument flawlessly. She works harder than the others around her. She picks up extra work when needed. Yet, she is invisible in the organization. Her peer, who joined three months after Geeta and is equally good at her work as Geeta, lately got promoted to senior associate attorney, a position Geeta was working toward. When Geeta approached me for coaching, it was visible to me that Geeta could not self-promote and talk about her work.

DOI: 10.4324/9781003439134-15

Another client, Sandy, is the marketing director at an advertising firm in Paris. Sandy previously worked as a senior manager in another firm in Paris and quit her job two months ago. She says her aspirations and ambitions were high, but the company failed to notice her. During the coaching sessions, she understood that the company failed to see her because Sandy never made herself visible.

And it's not only women. Men go unnoticed, too.

Bryan directed some of the best theater plays in Singapore. His plays were always well-scripted, and the audience loved the actor's performances. Yet, his income wasn't where it should have been.

Suresh is an IT leader who puts his best foot forward daily at work. He comes with a strong work ethic, contributes valuable ideas, and always makes a positive impact. While he was vying for the C.I.O. role, the position went to someone from outside the company. On checking with his boss about what made them choose another candidate over him, who has been with the company for more than eleven years, he said that the board referred them to this candidate's great ability at problem-solving under tight deadlines. Well, the answer surprised Suresh because, on many occasions, Suresh has proven his ability to problem-solve under tight deadlines.

All of these real-life incidences of my clients point us in one direction: getting noticed by the top management. Sadly, in a noisy, competitive corporate world, you must do more than simply work hard. However, self-promotion doesn't come quickly. Humans cling to an outmoded assumption that our achievements will speak for themselves, so we often hold back from verbalizing our achievements and goals to our employers.

Being noticed at work means your boss and other higher-ups recognize your contributions. Maybe they see you're great at problem-solving under tight deadlines, or that you share valuable industry knowledge with your colleagues, or for task execution or day-to-day behavior, like constant compassion and support for coworkers.

And getting noticed is the toughest for most professionals because we fall short of self-promotion. It's hard for anyone to speak volumes about themselves and their work. Most of us give a 110% to our work, but we talk about it only 10% and only 40% gets noticed at the top. The remaining 60% of your efforts and work tend to go unnoticed.

If you aspire to climb higher in this modern and competitive climate, you'll need a sponsor as well, someone who will amplify your work to the broader workplace.

A sponsor will use their internal political and social capital to advance their career within an organization. Behind closed doors, they will argue your case. Sponsors help you *move* up.

Your work must be recognized to succeed and make it to the top. If your career is moving forward, chances are a behind-the-scenes sponsor pulls strings on your behalf.

HOW DO YOU ATTRACT A SPONSOR?

It's one of the most frequently asked questions. And my answer is that you don't find sponsors – you attract them. And you attract them not just inside your company but from the outside too. You never get to choose the sponsor; the sponsor almost always chooses you. How does that happen?

Well, for you to attract a sponsor, you have to focus more on three significant pillars of success (Figure P8.1).

PILLAR OF UNIQUENESS   PILLAR OF RELATIONSHIP   PILLAR OF EXCELLENCE

FIGURE P8.1
Three significant pillars of success.

1. Pillar of Excellence

People will find out when you consistently deliver an excellent product and give that extra 0.5%. I like what Michael Jordan said, "Let your game be your promotional or marketing tool." You must go beyond our job description, beyond what is expected of you, and deliver above everyone else around you. That gets you noticed. Simple things like arriving early and leaving late, signing up for voluntary activities at work, initiating new ideas, asking questions, and staying relevant in your field. Lata Mangeshkar has been one of the strongest pillars of the Indian film industry. In the early era of filmmaking, most singers chose to excel only in one. She went on to learn and record songs in various languages, which were out of her comfort zone. She went the extra mile and delivered excellently, which no signer of her era did. Going the extra mile is vital to being noticed by a sponsor. Because when you provide excellence, you send out strong signals that the sponsor can use their political and social influence to speak about you. You are gaining their credibility. You are letting them know that they can count on you and that advocating for you will improve their credibility, too. Putting in the extra 0.5% and outperforming others creates the excellence that speaks for itself. Excellence is not a position – it's a movement! Excellence is your intention to do better tomorrow than you're already doing today. Delivering with excellence means redefining existing performance standards and challenging existing paradigms of world best practices.

2. Pillar of Relationships

If I were to name just one ingredient that would help anyone be successful at their workplace, it would be the ability to get along with people. Theodore Roosevelt said, "The most important single ingredient in the success formula is knowing how to get along with people." Harvard conducted a famous study spanning eighty years. They found that relationships, not money or fame, led to people living long and happy lives.

I want to emphasize that the investment that you make in people, engaging and conversing with them, allows them to know you better. Ultimately, business and work are all about the human bond. Relationships, I believe, should be such that they always lead to a win–win for all. Never keep a scorecard of your relationships; never be manipulative in building relations. Genuine love and appreciation for people will take you a long way in getting someone to advocate for you. People want to know that you are real. That you are trustworthy. Your success expands or contracts based on your relationships.

3. Pillar of Uniqueness

I've always felt the pressure to fit in. There's always been a gap between what I want to be and what the world thinks I should be. But the pressure to fit in and be liked turned me into a social chameleon. I tried to be the person I felt I should be to blend in with those around me. I started speaking on the stage as an American would. I started dressing to fit in the culture. The more I listened to, abided by, and fueled these stereotypes, the more they defined me. And then, despite working harder than anyone around me, I still was not getting where I wanted to be until one day, I sat and asked myself: *What makes me different? How would I like to be remembered? The answers to these questions helped me bring out my uniqueness.*

SEPARATE YOURSELF FROM THE HERD AND GET NOTICED

I see many of us in the corporate world trying to fit in. We hide our uniqueness. We compare ourselves to others. We think of who we should be rather than being who we are. And so we miss out on bridging our unique talents and abilities on the table.

Develop your signature and dare to be different. It is very imperative to brand yourself and carry your flag. You must be able to position yourself differently. Sponsors are rarely attracted to people with a herd mentality. The red waters are crowded, and sponsors are not looking there for anyone. Nelson Mandela did not imitate Gandhi's brand of nonviolence. He built his uniqueness as a leader. What do you want to be known for? A sponsor is attracted to your reputation, the values you stand for, your identity, and your distinctiveness as a leader. Daring to be unique, you will engage your teams, build support from your suppliers, and strengthen your proposition in the organization. People who break the mold and create an advantage for themselves, their team, and the organization are often noticed well. Have the courage to be different.

Now let me tell you something. The right people around you must notice your work. So, how do you identify a sponsor? You will need to check on three things:

1. Who is influential when it comes to the decision-making table?
2. Do they have exposure to your work?
3. Who in power is supporting you the most?

Getting the endorsement of someone with real influence goes a long way, regardless of your industry. To make it to the top, you must have someone who talks so positively about you behind your back and uses their clout to help you advance in your career. Their endorsement can result in significant career gains, like promotions, raises, or bonuses – or help you land the opportunities that lead to those more significant milestones, like spearheading a new project or taking on a plum assignment.

Doing great, working hard, or consistently delivering outstanding performance does not guarantee the next level you aim for. You need to be noticed and ensure you effectively manage those in power – which requires going above your ego and making them feel good about themselves.

Remember, people who are influencers in your organization and those in higher positions are too busy with their agendas and jobs. Such people aren't paying that much attention to you and what you are doing. So don't assume that your boss knows what you are doing and your accomplishments. For you to reach the top, those in a position of power have to choose you for the senior role.

I once worked very closely with the chief marketing officer of a company in Bangalore. He would always say to his team that ad recall is one of the most prominent measures of effectiveness in marketing. Does your consumer remember and recall the ad and product? The same holds true for each of us. Do your seniors and influencers recall you and your work when decisions about you are made in rooms where you are absent? Are you memorable to them?

Most people go unnoticed in the organization because they do things only to maintain a positive self-image in the company and be liked by everyone. In the bargain, they fail to do the most significant things. So get over yourself and get beyond your concern for self-image. Be comfortable in your skin.

When we are comfortable in our own skin, we are not fighting against or with anyone, as we've discovered our true nature and live by it. We are courageous enough to live our truth. Have the boldness to go into your industry and create value never created.

LEADERSHIP CHALLENGE

Begin to attract the right sponsors by developing the pillars of excellence, relationship, and uniqueness.

Power 9

Sow and Reap Continuously

In my workshops, I often ask leaders if they have a deep-rooted career aspiration. The room is full of hands rising high up, indicating that I am in a room of achievers. Some aspire to get to the C-Suite level, some want to be great leaders, and others want to create something impactful.

However, not many of them will fulfill their aspiration. I say this out of more than fifteen years of coaching leaders globally. I have seen many leaders' aspirations go unfulfilled.

Why? Because many will give up on their aspirations.

One of the laws that benefited me greatly in my career and helped me move ahead is the law of sow and reap, with more emphasis on sowing.

Have you heard the parable of the sower?

A farmer went out to sow his seeds? Some fell along the path as he was scattering the source, and the birds came and ate them up. Some fell on rocky places where they did not have much soil. They sprang up quickly because the soil was shallow. But the plants were scorched and withered when the sun came up because they had no roots.

Other seeds fell among thorns, which grew up but were choked by the plants. Still other seeds fell on good soil, producing a crop – a 100, 60, or 30 times what was sown.

The point of the story' is twofold – one is that the seeds being sown can only take root and grow into a vigorous plant if the soil has been adequately prepared to receive them. Thus, we should take great care to see where we are sowing.

Second, if we were to change the story's focus from the soil to the sower? The sower's job is to spread the seed.

DOI: 10.4324/9781003439134-16

Some of that seed is wasted, though, falling on the hardened path or among the weeds and thorns. Watching the birds eat up the seed and fly away must be a little disheartening for the sower.

Sometimes, you might wonder, "What's the point?" or "Is this worth it?" But look at the sower. He does not stop. He perseveres with the usual sense of urgency. He is the sower.

Have you stopped seeding specific "fields" in your career? What can you do to redouble your efforts?

As leaders, you are a sower. When you put seeds in the ground, these are your dreams, visions, aspirations, and hopes. You can sow the seed of wanting to climb the corporate ladder, of leading with impact, of being an innovator … whatever your seeds are, you start sowing them today.

Some of these seeds will wither away, some will be eaten by the birds who are your competitors and haters, but many will fall on fertile ground.

As you nourish these seeds on the fertile ground daily, in time to come, maybe after a year, three, or five years, those seeds will start to sprout.

So what you want to do in life is to sow the seeds and nourish them continually.

Have you intentionally sown your seeds on the proper fertile grounds for your career?

Think about the types of seeds you have been sowing. Are you sowing encouragement, hope, blessing, and love? Then that's what you'll reap in the future. But if you've been sowing criticism, judgment, and anger, you're probably already reaping a bad harvest.

It's time to start observing and changing your seed.

This is the practice of "sow and harvest," where if one puts in the best efforts to give themselves the best education, training, and coaching today, one shall definitely see results being achieved in times to come.

And as you sow the seeds of your aspirations, there will come a season where you feel nothing is happening; there is no growth, change, or harvest. It is not easy to keep doing the right things, especially when there is no sign that anybody in the organization appreciates it and no evidence of any good effect.

Remember this, my friend: there is always a time lag between the seed going into the ground and the harvest coming out. The farmer never knows, early on, how the weather may affect the crop or even if the seed will germinate. But if he does not sow, inevitably, he will not reap.

The harvest cannot happen without sowing first; we are as good as the efforts that we put in.

THE MIRACLES OF THE HARVEST

In times when you do not see any harvest, you want to dig in your heels and stay put, continuing to harvest and nourish in the suitable soil.

You are never given a timetable for when your dreams and your vision will come to pass.

When I was in school, my dad often reminded me that when we truly wish for something, the universe hears it, packs it for us, and ships it to us. However, that package does not have a delivery date on it. So, you must stay in faith and keep sowing the seed of your dream until your package is delivered.

His statement was reaffirmed in my school's church, where the father often told us during school assembly that God says if you plant the seed, I will make the tree. God says, "Leave the miracle part to me. I've got the seed, the soil, the sunshine, the rain, and the seasons. I'm God, and all this miraculous stuff is easy for me. I have reserved something very special for you, and that is to plant the seed."

I have found in life that if you want a miracle, you first need to do whatever it is you can do – if that's to plant, then plant; if it is to read, then read; if it is to change, then change; if it is to work, then work; whatever you have to do. And then the miracles will be on their way.

Great leaders do not give up on their vision, people, and organization. That's how they make it to the top.

A leader is in the position of sowing many seeds. You can sow seeds of belonging, empowerment, togetherness, purpose, love and affection, vision, team building, change and innovation, trust, and better work relationships. Be intentional about what seeds you sow and where you sow them.

Being out of sync with time and place is why many leaders fail to reach the top. The scripture tells us that "whoever sows sparingly will also reap sparingly, and whoever sows generously will also reap generously."

If you do little to no work, you will have little to no growth as a leader. You will succeed as a leader with great effort and practice. You will reap what you sow.

ROUTINE AND CONSISTENCY IS WHAT IT'S ALL ABOUT

Robert Collier said that success is the sum of small efforts, repeated day in and day out. Routine and consistency is what it's all about. The work comes every day. What decisions you make daily and how you act daily are what matters.

I once was asked how I get the time to write my books with my hectic schedule. Well, it's never about writing the book; it's about writing one page daily. That's consistency. I wake up every day at 5.00 am and write. That''s routine.

Could a daily routine be what's missing in your success equation? Is it possible that the key to changing your results is hidden within a structure of sameness?

More important than the end result is your daily action, your sowing.

Leadership takes hardwork. As you sow these seeds, life will always pay the price you ask of it. You have dreams and aspirations in your career life, whatever they may be; maybe you want to become the director, vice president, C.E.O., or an entrepreneur; life will ask you to pay the price of hardwork, failure, patience, and sacrifice. And let me tell you, the price you will pay for not making your dream come true is far greater than you will pay to make it come true.

Those who make it to the top in the field are the ones who sow daily. Someone has worthily quoted, "Today is the father of tomorrow." What we are today and how we will be tomorrow result from what we have been yesterday. This principle is irrevocable, for nobody can escape from its certainty. The best is to understand this adage and ingrain it in our everyday work to ensure that what we sow today is with an eye to the future.

The cost is hardwork, where those who have made it to the top have reaped the fruits of labor cultivated on the hard bed of perseverance. If we noticed their hardwork, we would realize it was all their daily sowing.

I tell all of my coaching clients that when they practice each day what I teach them during the coaching sessions, is when they will see a transformation within months to come. They will not wake up the day after the session and see the transformation. Not at all. When they practice the techniques every day, they will see the change.

Your career is a reflection of the seed you sowed yesterday. And what we sow today determines what we will reap tomorrow. An unintentional sower will reap unwanted fruit, whereas a sower who sows according to the potential harvest they see will sow with purpose.

Your seed of sowing determines your harvest. We will always reap a harvest on what we sow.

Sowing seeds does not mean you harvest the next day. Today, most people want to sow and harvest immediately. A giant oak tree is outside my mom's home in Mumbai, India. Last month, when I visited my mom's house, I looked at how large that old tree had become since I saw it as a kid.

It's incredible to think that that gigantic tree was merely a tiny seed at one point. Harvest happens at its time and in its season. Diligent leaders never give up on sowing just because they aren't seeing the harvest soon. They keep sowing and nourishing the seeds they've planted.

And when the time is right, know how to leverage and harvest those seeds.

Many people are afraid to reap what they have sown. We build great relationships; we nourish them but never leverage them because we feel we are being manipulative. I believe that we are helping each other when we leverage our relations. We are interconnected human beings. We are dependent on each other. So harvest your seeds of relationships, talents, and skills at the right time.

My friend, you are continually sowing, whether conscious of it or not. By the thoughts that you think, by how you feel, and by the acts you perform. And that's the beauty of it. You can always choose what you want to show. The possibilities are endless.

It makes me think of a famous verse in the Bible: "There is a time for everything and a season for every activity under heaven."

Many fail because they are out of sync with time and place. They plant in the wrong season. They plant before they plan. They try to harvest before the fruit is ripe.

Many of us remain mediocre in our careers and do not reach the top because we see that the lack of success in a few attempts is a failure, and we stop trying.

The other day, while watching the Discovery Channel with my two girls, the report talked about how lions only succeed in a quarter of their hunting attempts— – which means they fail in 75% and succeed in only 25%. Despite this small percentage most predators share, they don't despair in their pursuit and hunting attempts.

The main reason for this is not because of hunger, as some might think, but the understanding of the "Law of Wasted Efforts" that has been instinctively built into animals, a law in which nature is governed. Half of the eggs of fish are eaten … half of the baby bears die before puberty … most of the world's rains fall in oceans … and most of the seeds of trees are eaten by birds. Scientists have found that animals, trees, and other forces of nature are more receptive to the law of "wasted efforts."

So, as you work toward the top, there will be many failures, and you will feel that most of your efforts are wasted. Rather than giving up, remind yourself of this law of wasted efforts. The fact is that the more we try, the more we are likely to be successful. No matter how many times you fail, you can still be successful. Our success is the result of our efforts and attempts.

A good day is judged by the seeds you sow. "Keep sowing!"

Keep sowing your seed, for you never know which will grow – perhaps it all will.

LEADERSHIP CHALLENGE

Sow seeds of growth and success daily through your persistent actions. Don't give up.

Power 10

Play Big

I don't know how you found this book, but I do know why you are here. You are here because some of you want to play a bigger game.

Years ago, I wasn't known for having trained and coached a million professionals through my work. I was a leadership instructor, and I would do training for small groups of 10–15 people at a time. I was earning well, not excellent, but good enough. And I was satisfied with my life, living the American dream and traveling around.

One day, while traveling to San Francisco for work, my connecting flight was from Charlotte. At the airport, I met Alex, the C.E.O. of the company I once worked for. We shook hands, and he asked, "Payal, how are you doing, and what's taking you to San Francisco?"

"Alex, I am traveling to SFO to conduct a seminar on leadership for around fifteen people," I enthusiastically replied. "That's nice, so how much will you make in this session," came his next question. "Oh," I responded smilingly, "around seven hundred and fifty dollars." "So Payal," he said, looking a little concerned, "I am sure you are traveling business class, aren't you?" I'll be honest: this question took me aback, and I hesitantly responded negatively, saying that I travel coach class.

Alex looked at me and said, "Payal, why are you doing this?" And just as he completed his question, I got defensive, and I am sure he saw it on my face. In a slightly raised voice, I said that I didn't care about the money or whether I could travel business class or not, and that I just love what I do.

Alex smiled and asked me to sit, and what he said next made me introspect a great deal. He said:

> Payal, this is not what I meant. I have known you for more than seven years now. I have seen your dedication and passion for your work. What I am

DOI: 10.4324/9781003439134-17

saying is that you are great at leadership. You have this awesome concept of Success Within leadership methodology. You know how to get people to build on their inner leadership competencies. Why, then, are you playing small? You are comfortable teaching small groups of fifteen to twenty people, whereas the program can benefit more than a million people in the workforce. Payal, I want you to think big and think bold.

As he was completing his sentence, there was an announcement for his flight, and he wished me luck as he went to board his flight.

Throughout my flight to SFO and back home to North Carolina, I sat silently, reflecting on what he said. And the two words that struck me were "play big," "play bold." It just made me realize that I was playing small. And I decided I would no longer teach only thirty people in a small room.

I began thinking about how to go from thirty to three hundred to three thousand before I completed training and coaching one million plus people to become world-class leaders.

Many of us, like me, play small in our careers. We take every step with caution. We stay satisfied with what we have – focused on short-term, temporary comfort, security, relief, and validation. Playing small means our actions are motivated by our fears, insecurities, low self-worth, and scarcity.

A 2019 Gallup Survey showed that only 15% of global full-time workers are fully engaged. That means, in essence, 85% have little to no passion for what they do for most of their day.

In contrast, leaders who play big are the ones who never stay satisfied with what they have. They stretch themselves and are willing to take risks. They exist in a high-performance state where they live up to their true capability and aspirations.

How do these leaders play big? They focus on two significant elements:

1. Purpose

I've been asked this one enjoyable question time and again. "Payal, I get very overwhelmed when I think of long-term goals. Is setting a long-term goal necessary?" Well, the answer is both YES and NO.

Many leaders believe that for career success, setting long-term goals is necessary. They hear great motivational speeches, feel the dopamine rush in their body, and begin working toward that long-term goal. And midway, many get tired, feel overwhelmed, and give up. For instance, Charles, one of my very old coaching clients, set a long-term goal to get into a C-Suite role. He worked hard toward it and within eleven years, he got tired of everything and was unable to get anywhere close to his goal; he gave up as he reached the director position.

And then there were some excellent excuses he gave for not making it to where he wanted, such as money and position aren't everything, work–life balance is getting disrupted, getting into C-Suite means playing politics, and I am not interested in it, and the list goes on.

Prevailing leadership wisdom claims that setting specific, actionable goals is the best way to achieve what we want – getting to the next level, building a successful business, and becoming a great leader.

For many of us, this is how we approach our career, too, and we are in some way like Charles, where excuses become a part of our lives, and we feel comfortable blaming our failures on destiny.

Goals are essential, but you must take a different and more significant approach to advance your career. Before setting goals, set a purpose. The purpose is more important than your goals. Goals are a way to reach something deeper and more fulfilling in your career. It will constantly inspire you and allow you to overcome all challenges. Rarely do people with a purpose give up because it gives their work meaning. Everyone has a purpose. But don't actively look for purpose in your life because the harder you try, the harder it can be to find.

Remember chasing butterflies as a kid? The more you ran, the more they flew to escape you. But sometimes, when you just sat on the grass and watched, they'd come to rest on your shoulder.

Finding purpose in your work can be very much like this. Don't run trying to find meaning in your career. Instead, do a quiet introspection and some soul search.

2. Systems

Leaders who play big and think extensively set systems. It's a process I've taught many of my clients to help them scale their careers.

For instance, once you've figured out your purpose, chunk it down into goals. If you want to become a company director or leave corporate life to become an entrepreneur, these are your goals and ambitions. How you will achieve this goal is a system you build. Goals tell you where you want to go; they focus on tomorrow.

Systems tell you what you need to do daily to get there; they're focused on today. They tell you how you achieve your goals.

To play big, you must build a system to get there. Systems are always scalable.

"How will you make arriving at your destination (your goal) easy?" It's a question you must ask yourself once you set your purpose.

Systems are the building blocks for success. It is a process, a method, of action that keeps you on track and produces a consistent and measurable result.

Your system will have many inbuilt elements. Here is a quick equation to remember.

Systems=(Intention+Effort+Focus+Clarity+BluePrint+Awareness+ Commitment)

GET OUT OF "BED" AND GRAB THE "OAR"

Life throws things at us when we least expect them; some things are great, and others are difficult. Watching the difference in people's reactions and how some individuals can find good in anything while others fall apart when difficult circumstances arise is fascinating.

We all have days when we wake up and want the day to end. That's the day we seem to have one problem after another when we get there. Choosing not to fall when things don't go to plan or a curve ball rolls out in front of us when least expected is what makes you a meta-leader and reach the top.

Many people don't jumpstart their lives because they have nothing to jump to! They get pushed from one job to another – one department to another, one role to another, and every day, they operate in a mode of survival, fearing job loss and facing insecurities. They get tired of their work and soon begin to hate their jobs.

Having a purpose gives you direction in your life. You are the only person who can steer the wheel of your career-life. But many of us prefer to let someone else drive our career life.

I remember once, during an introductory coaching call with Sandeep, he told me that he had asked many of his people in high positions in companies what he should do in his career. Everyone gave him different advice, which left him confused. When he asked me the same question, "Payal, what should I do in my career?" I gave him an exercise to do to help him introspect and get the answers from within. He needed to be in the driver's seat and steer the wheel of his career life.

Have you watched the German movie, *Silent Revolution?* The movie highlights that old thinking patterns, working models, and management practices which are widely spread among bigger companies are not suitable anymore. It requires courage to challenge our old thinking and working models and try a completely different approach.

Questions like how to deal with our challenges, how to use our resources in a sustainable way, or how to help people and employees to unfold their full potential, are questions the movie tries to answer.

The reason I mentioned this movie here is to bring forth the point that when we change the way we think, we begin to play big in our career life. To make it to the top, you cannot work with old thinking patterns with which you have become comfortable.

Most people prefer to spend more time sleeping than visualizing their dreams. That is why most people are not living a successful life.

If you want to be successful, you must spend time envisioning the things you want to accomplish. That's when you will get out of bed and grab the oar.

We are all born to play big. You are powerful beyond measure. We must honor our talents, resources, and gifts to the best of our ability. I invite you to overcome your fears and push past your resistance as you leap forward. Ultimately, the money and success that genuinely last come not to those who focus on goals but to those who focus on their purpose and play big in their career.

LEADERSHIP CHALLENGE

Begin to think of your deep-end purpose and build a scalable system for you to reach the top.

Power 11

The Devil Is in the Feedback

I love playing golf. I am still in the initial learning phase of the game. My instructor taught me the importance of the proper follow-through to perfect their drives and putts. Without it, golfers don't make their shots or perform optimally.

Leaders need to take the same approach when it comes to feedback. Essentially, no task is complete, no objective is reached, and no successes can be experienced unless – and until – feedback has been given and received.

You might agree that providing feedback has long been considered an essential skill for leaders. And most leaders do that well.

The problem comes in when leaders want feedback.

Most people suggest going on for *360-degree feedback*. I don't advocate this.

Having coached numerous leaders globally and across various industries, I can almost guarantee that there is a fundamental problem with all types of 360-degree feedback. And the problem is that these are time-consuming, limited, and need more authenticity to help you improve.

Why?

Well, because people aren't willing to say the real thing to the leaders, and number two, you aren't ready to accept genuine feedback. So, before you go out there to get some authentic feedback, you need to ask yourself two questions:

(1) Why do I want the feedback? (2) Do I really want to improve?

As an executive coach, I work with many successful leaders who want to become even more effective. Recently, I asked a client of mine what kind

     DOI: 10.4324/9781003439134-18

of feedback she was receiving to help her be a better leader. She said, "My last performance review was really positive. My boss told me I'm doing a great job and should just continue doing what I'm doing."

This type of feedback will never help you improve your game. To make it to the top, you will need people to tell you upfront where the problem in you is. You want honest feedback that helps you improve and gets you to do some work inside yourself.

Ranjana, the regional director for an international preschool, was having dinner with Anil, her boss, on a trip together to Singapore. They were going there to discuss some critical team issues popping up frequently at the head office in Bangalore in Anil's team. Ranjana used this private opportunity to give Anil some feedback.

"Anil, you are more task-oriented than people-oriented." Ranjana said. "You often focus on the project rather than your people's needs. The team needs your authentic leadership."

The timing of this feedback couldn't have been better. Tomorrow's meeting was intended to address the misalignment among Anil's team.

The feedback worked. During the meeting with the senior management team in Singapore Anil did some brainstorming and whiteboard to drive at the best possible solution, keeping in mind the blind spots that Ranjana helped him with.

We need feedback if we want to learn how to do anything better. In my mind, Anil is a fortunate leader. He had a direct report from Rajnana that was candid and who was courageous enough to give him feedback.

Most leaders don't want honest feedback, so they never ask for it.

If you want genuine feedback, you must create a safe environment for your people to share feedback. Most of the time, your direct reports face what I call "the feedback fear" where they hesitate to mention any of your improvement areas openly.

In my experience, there are a hundred ways to ask for feedback. We ask people, "What do you think of me?" "How do you feel about my work?" "What do you hate about me?" or "What do you like about me?" Think about it. How many of them want to express their "true" feelings about you to you? No one wants to be called judgmental. No one would like to be criticized later for what they said about you.

You can get authentic feedback from almost anyone on your team by asking a simple question during your 1:1 with them.

What can I do better as your leader?

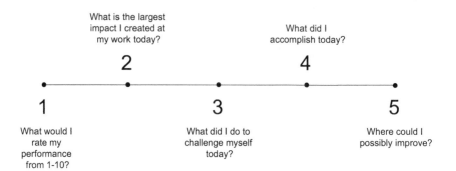

FIGURE P11.1
Five step reflection process.

Simple, direct questions like these make your team feel that their opinion is important to you. They feel privileged to be asked, and most of the time, you will get authentic feedback.

Now, along with getting feedback externally, you must develop the ability to give yourself accurate feedback. This is called self-reflection.

Most of us rely too much on external validation and feedback. Your success depends on how well you know yourself (Figure P11.1).

5-STEP SELF-REFLECTION PROCESS

Rate your progress:

#1 What would I rate my performance from 1–10?
#2 What is the most significant impact I created at my work today?
#3 What did I do to challenge myself today?
#4 What did I accomplish today?
#5 Where could I possibly improve?

Once you ask yourself these questions, the next important step is to reflect. Just like all other forms of feedback, for self-feedback to be helpful, it must be heard and valued.

Now, act upon the answers you get for your self-improvement.

The higher up you go in the organization, the more critical it is to get external and internal feedback. Your performance, results, and confidence will grow, and who doesn't want those things?

LEADERSHIP CHALLENGE

Each quarter, ask your management, your team, and yourself. What can I do better as a leader?

Power 12

Train Your Brain to Say No

This is a universal problem I've observed in both men and women, but more in women. People find it difficult to say NO when asked to work on something or take extra. And later, they repent.

The reason you aren't able to say no is that, number one, you don't value your time, goal, and energy; number two, you have what I call attention and approval-seeking disorder (A.A.S.D.); and number three, you are insecure about your job and position.

Raina wanted to become the C.E.O. of a nonprofit organization after retiring from her current job. She was already 49 years old, only ten years from her retirement, but was nowhere seemingly close to what she wanted. When I asked her why she wasn't utilizing her weekends to work toward what she ultimately wanted, she responded, "I do not have a minute. I am super busy with my day-to-day work at the office."

When I sat with Raina for her coaching sessions, I observed one of her behaviors that came her way, which was her inability to say no. And so she asked for everything on her plate, which she couldn't digest because she said yes more often than not; she had no margin space for her growth and dreams.

I issued a challenge that made her quite uncomfortable: during the next two weeks, I asked her to practice what I have taught many executives, the "Refrain and Reframe" strategy.

In yet another case, a very close friend of mine, Jay, the chief people officer at a well-known company in Kentucky, would often miss family get-togethers and keep friends waiting endlessly on dates to meet. Family and friends stayed away from him because of his lack of commitment to them. They felt undervalued and ignored by him. He was on the verge of getting a divorce from his wife. Jay was just everywhere at work. Whatever would

 DOI: 10.4324/9781003439134-19

happen at work, he just had to be there. He would often stretch himself to accommodate everyone's requests at work. He would be there for every meeting and would barely say no to anyone at work. Every time I met with him, I found him drained and tired. He was constantly rushing around to fulfill personal commitments.

I spoke to him about the "Refrain and Reframe" strategy that soon improved his life.

REFRAIN AND REFRAME

Most of us are unable to say no at work. We keep adding projects to our plates. We feel our presence is essential everywhere. We believe we should do everything, which will help us reach the next level.

When you practice the "Refrain and Reframe," it will help you create margin space in your life. You will be more productive, you will have time to do more significant projects, and you will become more creative and innovative.

Here's how the "Refrain and Reframe" strategy works.

When someone or something demands your time, refrain from immediately responding with a yes to any request. Instead, respond with something like, "I need to look at what else is on my calendar because I want to make sure I can fully commit to this request. I will get back to you in a day."

Next, reframe your thinking. Rather than feeling guilty and worried about saying no, use that space between the request and the response to consider a few essential items: whether you have time, the worst-case scenario if you declined, and whether you feel the task is necessary. Also, consider examining your relationship with the requester because sometimes relationships matter when denying requests.

The simple strategy helped her become more confident about herself and be more assertive toward knowing when and where to say no. All of this with two weeks of practice.

You can do it, too, using the refrain and reframe strategy.

A typical day at work for many of us might look like this: You're in the middle of a phone meeting when a message pops up on your laptop that your boss wants an urgent document. As you're trying to handle the phone meeting and send that document to your boss, a colleague stops by your desk, asking you to help solve an employee problem. When you get off the phone and send the document to your boss, you are about to help your colleague when a reminder pops up that it's time for the staff meeting. Most of us have a hectic day every day! We wake up to run in the race and sleep to wake up again and get back into the race.

Do you want to feel energetic? Do you want to be open-minded, achieve more, and stay motivated? Are you looking to enhance efficiency, balance mood, increase memory function, reduce tension and stress, flush out unwanted thoughts, have excellent work relations, expand your business, and speed up your growth?

If you answered yes to a few or all of these questions, you want to ensure you keep a margin space in your everyday life. Margin space is that little space held for contingencies or unanticipated situations. It's the space where you continue to reflect and work on developing yourself. It's the space you assign for your growth. The refrain and reframe strategy gives you that margin you desperately need.

We work in a closed compartment with no space at all. But guess what? Energy flows best between open spaces. And this should propel you to ask yourself, is there space in my life? The best way to simplify your life is to create space. To generate that margin space, you've got to be willing to say "No Thanks" to activities that don't advance your priorities.

SAY YES TO WHAT MATTERS MOST TO YOU

Many of us feel guilty about saying no. Maybe you're afraid of disappointing someone. Perhaps you're anxious to turn down your boss. Or maybe you're a people pleaser. No matter the reasons, learning to say no is essential to reaching the top. Most of us are raised to believe that saying no is terrible, making it difficult to say no at work, too.

Sometimes, we say no to the wrong things, such as great projects and opportunities. This happens when you doubt yourself. With imposter syndrome, you feel like you will not deliver the best. When you apply the refrain and reframe strategy, you begin to feel more confident from the inside.

By saying yes when you wish to say no, you are saying a big no to your dreams and goals. I have innumerable instances where I have said no because I knew it would take away time from my main agenda. It simply comes down to a straightforward question: Are you going to choose you or them?

Akash was seen everywhere around. He will show up if you need someone for a corporate social responsibility activity. If an offsite was planned and he was informed at the last minute about it, he would show up at the offsite. If his team had a game night organized and wanted Akash to be there, he would be there.

Akash said he was supportive and served them well as a leader. In reality, his people took him for granted. Not only did it make him appear familiar, but the management did not see him as the best candidate for the next role.

It is easy to say yes to every request on your time when the priorities of your life are unclear. When your days are not guided by an inspiring purpose for your future, you end up on everyone's agenda.

The solution is to be ultra clear about what your career purpose is.

The Chinese sage Chuang-tzu told the story of a man who forged swords for a maharaja. Even at 90, his work was carried out with exceptional precision and ability. No matter how rushed he was, he never made the slightest slip. One day, the maharaja asked the old man, "Is this a natural talent, or is there some special technique you use to create remarkable results?"

"It is concentration on the essentials," replied the sword crafter. "I took to forging swords when I was 21 years old. I did not care about anything else. I did not look at it or pay attention if it was not a sword. Forging swords became my passion and my purpose. I took all the energy I did not give in other directions and put it in the direction of my art, which is the secret to my mastery."

When everything feels urgent and essential, everything seems equal. We become active and busy, but this doesn't move us closer to success.

Many of us become so consumed with the micro activities of our work that we forget to focus on the macro activities, and then we begin to say yes to everyone and everything.

Michael Jordan, the best basketball player in history, did not negotiate his contracts, design his uniforms, and prepare his travel schedules. He focused his time and energy on what he did best: playing basketball.

Great leaders consciously train their brains to say no by clearly stating what they want to accomplish. Then, they direct all their energy and resources to achieve that. They are conscious of their capabilities.

They say yes to the right things using the refrain and reframe technique.

Learning to say no to the nonessentials will give you more time to devote to the things that can genuinely improve your career. Our mental fitness suffers when we bite off more than we can chew.

Saying no can benefit your performance and career. Being assertive pays off. It's essential for your mental well-being.

LEADERSHIP CHALLENGE

Be conscious of how often you say yes when you want to say no.

Power 13

Go for the Impossible

"You can achieve anything, and it's possible" is a phrase I grew up with. My dad instilled this message in me in the early years of my life. And at that time, I believed in this message with all my heart and soul.

But somewhere in the noise of corporate America, this message took a back seat. Somewhere, I began setting limits for myself. I believed there were limits to what I could do. I felt there were limits to the opportunities I could get, and soon, these limits became my reality. These limits began the day I got my first job description and key performance indicators (K.P.I.s) in the company I joined early in my career. And from there on, with every new role and a new company, I never dared to attempt anything outside of my job description. I only worked as hard to accomplish my KPIs.

Back then, I forgot that the job description was someone else's projections based on the company's policy and legalities, and the KPIs were what the company's expectation of me was. The person drafting these doesn't know my limitless potential.

How many of us limit ourselves based on our titles, positions, and job descriptions?

People who make it to the top of their field are not limited by their K.P.I.s.

Your mind is capable of achieving remarkable things. And wherever your mind goes, that's where your body's energy will follow.

I once had the opportunity to witness the Paralympics event in Qatar. There, I was awed at the high level of performance and optimism of the Paralympians. You could feel they are made to achieve anything despite their physical limitations. They can achieve the impossible.

Personally, I began to consciously remind myself of what my father would often tell me: "You can achieve anything, and it's possible."

When you genuinely believe you can achieve anything possible, your mind begins to find ways to get you there. Where we are is the totality of possibilities. We can either build walls of limitations around us or bridges of faith and belief.

IT ALL BEGINS IN THE MIND

One of the most valuable instruments the universe has blessed humans with is our mind. No one was believed to have run a mile in less than 4 minutes. It was impossible. But Roger Bannister proved everyone wrong. He was the first man to run a mile in under 4 minutes. It was believed impossible to land on the moon, but it happened.

It is the mind that holds the majority of people back from going after what they truly want. We doubt ourselves and it's what paralyzes people from taking action. Once you break down those mental barriers that have imprisoned you, you will live differently; your perspective, activities, goals, plans, limits, and fears will disappear.

Believe in yourself. I believe in you. You are holding this book in your hand, reading it page by page because something inside of you tells you that you can achieve great things in your career.

Reaching the top means being able to do what no one else around you is doing. It's about achieving what no one else has. You must ask yourself this question daily: "Am I working to my fullest potential?" "Am I using the gifts and talents I've been blessed with to the best of my ability to achieve anything I want in my career?"

THE 4-STEP METHOD TO TRAIN YOUR MIND TO ACHIEVE THE IMPOSSIBLE

Now, when I say that you can achieve anything and it's possible, I want you to know that it requires work. It cannot magically happen. You have to program your mind for what you want.

1. Choose your "Mission Possible": We can achieve so much beyond what is expected of us at work. There are many problems to be solved in the business world. There are many innovations to be done. There is a lot

of change to be brought into our work environment. Each of us can do something which has never been done before. That's why we are here. So, find that one mission that you want to make possible. Don't debate and fret over the size of your task. All great things are big.

2. Observe your self-talk: All tremendous and mediocre things begin with self-talk. Begin to observe what's happening inside you and how you feel, react, and believe. Once, while driving my older daughter to her swim lessons, I heard someone on the radio say, "How you talk to yourself, about yourself, when by yourself, finally decides what you will achieve." I want you to let this sentence sink inside you just like it did in me. It's profound. Most of us talk negatively about ourselves, especially when by ourselves. This negative self-talk projects itself into your actions. And then we begin to play small. What if you stopped comparing yourself to others in your field and embraced your uniqueness? Can you imagine how much you could accomplish?

3. Improve your focus muscle: You can do anything you put your mind to. Where focus goes, energy flows is what I have always practiced. You need to get laser-focused on what you want and create a crystal-clear vision of where you want to go. Most people's focus is so dispersed that energy can never flow directly toward achieving their big goal.

4. Execute: One of the biggest challenges people face is execution. We all have big goals and dreams but lack execution. Reading books, attending conferences, or listening to motivational tapes are fantastic. But knowing how to translate your knowledge and plans into execution is the key. So many of us do not take action because we are overwhelmed by the how. All you need to do is take a leap of faith and take the following best action, and then from that space, take the following best action, and the journey continues. The results will be so powerful that your mind cannot fathom them. Taking action feels fantastic. Nothing happens until we put in the work, no matter how determined or how much information we obtain. This means we must roll up our sleeves and get our hands dirty.

SUCCESS HAS NO AGE LIMIT

There is inside you all of the potential to be whatever you want to be. Only you can limit that potential. Don't let your fears decide your career path.

Unfortunately, many people feel it's all over when they are in the prime of life. A classic example occurred once when I was on a call-in radio talk show. One caller was a gentleman who said, "Ms. Nanjiani, I'm fifty-two years old. I've never done anything significant in my career; now it's too late. It's all over."

As a coach, I have experienced many such conversations with people. I am reminded of what John Johnson said that men and women are limited not by the place of their birth, not by the color of their skin, but by the size of their hope. You can go from where you are to anywhere you want to go. But it will not be an easy journey. There will be the inevitable hills and valleys before you can go over the top. However, if you are full of hope and want to get there, the information you have at your disposal will supply the "how-to."

Alexander the Great accomplished more heroic deeds in his thirty-three years of life than most people could ever hope to dream of in their entire lifetime. He was undefeated in battle, conquered most of the known world, and is remembered today as one of the greatest and most successful generals in warfare. In his short lifetime, he carved out one of the largest land empires in the history of the world.

There is nothing impossible to him who will try, said Alexander the Great.

You will waste endless hours thinking and doing minor things and have no energy for significant tasks.

There is a story told of a thirsty donkey: on one side is hay and on the other is water. If he can't decide what he wants, he dies.

You have to go after what you want, or you will be confined to the life that you have stumbled into. Most people are confined to a life of mediocrity because they don't bother making a determined effort to pursue what they genuinely want to accomplish.

If you don't believe that you can become successful, then you will not take any action, and you will just continue doing the same mediocre things day after day, and you will never chase after your dreams.

You can do more than you know; develop yourself, start reprogramming your mind, and don't just settle for the so-called everyday normal career life.

This is your career, so you have to do what is right for you. Nobody else is going to hold our hand and take you there. To live on a new level, you must set your goals, see the vision, make plans, and take consistent daily action.

Consistency is vital. Many people want the good life but just give up after a few days, or they don't even try if you are truly serious about moving your life in a new direction, you need to take action every single damn day.

Believe in yourself. You have something to offer this world that nobody else does. When you have faith in yourself, you are instilled with the ability to make the right decisions without second-guessing your mind.

LEADERSHIP CHALLENGE

Think of that one thing you want to accomplish in the next 36 months. Take one small action right now to get started.

Power 14

Avoid Shiny Object Syndrome

"I have an excellent idea for a new business or product."

It's a statement I hear almost daily from leaders I coach, and it isn't necessarily a good thing.

Let me explain. I coach leaders with several years of experience in very senior roles. Shiny objects syndrome (S.O.S.) increases as you go up the corporate ladder. When someone with many years of experience comes to me, excited about a new product line or service, I can't help but approach the conversation a little guardedly, because it tells me they might have the S.O.S. – shiny objects syndrome – and it affects all leaders to some degree, even the most disciplined ones.

It's a disease of distraction. You're mindlessly jumping from one project to another, assuming each presents a more extensive, better option for you than the previous.

This rabbit life impacts many leaders. For instance, while coaching a senior vice president, we discussed how he needed to build his leadership brand. I saw how he couldn't decide on his niche, so he jumped from wanting to be a problem solver to being a great communicator to being known as an authority in tech – all within three months.

S.O.S. happens due to ambiguous guilt that there was something bigger, better, and more exciting to work on.

I've seen how mindlessly many leaders I coach jump from one job to another, leave their current job seduced by entrepreneurship, or hop from one idea to another.

So many of us have had the experience of listening to a motivational talk and suddenly making a connection between the speaker's big idea and a

DOI: 10.4324/9781003439134-21

challenge we face at work and then jumping out of the current project to chase a new one.

Shiny object syndrome is a condition that impacts millions of professionals when they get side-tracked by a new business idea or project that feels new and exciting.

I'm not saying every new project is a bad idea. The key is determining a good idea and what is just a shiny object meant to distract you from your goals. If you tend to follow an idea without first weighing its potential and get distracted from it soon, that's a problem. Too many leaders spin their wheels, running from one idea to the next without ever following through and achieving success in any area. And so the shiny object syndrome can be so seductive.

Many leaders are plagued with the S.O.S. When S.O.S. sets in, it forces you to chase project after project, and change after change, never settling with one option. Once they get there and see what the object is, they immediately lose interest and start chasing the next thing.

As new ideas occur to them, they will often share them without thinking them through.

And do you know when you are most prone to develop the S.O.S.? It's when you are overworked and stressed, when you are compared to others, or if you are a victim of fear of Missing Out.

Highly successful leaders practice being in the moment and working on what they have in front of them.

One day, while in a private meeting in the office of Kiara, the founder and C.E.O. of a paramedical company, for some meaningful discussions about coaching two of her highly critical leaders, her phone rang.

She ignored it.

After three rings, I looked at her and asked, *"Aren't you going to get that?"*

The C.E.O. paused and remarked, *"No. I don't know whether that call is important, but it can wait. I do know this meeting is important."*

Feeling valued, I got a big smile, and we continued the conversation with new energy.

Shiny objects like email, texts, unscheduled phone calls, conversations from the next cube, or in the hallway en route to meetings (many of which are shiny objects, in and of themselves). Oh, and let's not forget the Internet's siren and clicking on one too many *interesting* links that have little to do with our initial query (guilty as charged!). Some days are downright blinding by the glare and impeding our vision.

Avoiding the shiny object syndrome is no rocket science. Kiara simply focused on•the present moment and the present task.

Successful leaders avoid S.O.S. because they know that productivity takes a hit, too. It leads to an inability to finish projects, poor planning of your ideas and directives, confusing your staff, and you'll never get to see the long-term benefits of your current project.

IT'S TIME WE LOOK INWARDS, NOT OUTWARDS

Most of us want to stay the course. You can avoid the shiny object by internalizing and asking yourself whether you *really* need to be at that other place, doing something else as opposed to where you are, doing what you are doing.

When you have some goal out there you are stretching for and reaching for; you've got to stick to it if you want great results.

I started writing for school newsletters initially and then graduated to local newspapers, then to online and print magazines before I was invited by some of the top publishers in the world to write books for corporate leaders.

But I would never have been doing this had I fallen prey to the S.O.S. and if I hadn't been willing to stick to my purpose of helping leaders become the best version of themselves.

Listen to me, my friend; people will pull you in all directions. Add to this the information age we are in, and you will be blinded by objects that strongly urge you to leave the current thing at hand to try something new.

Scientists consider the ability to establish mental focus as a significant predictor of a person's future success.

If you're not focused and switch from one random activity to another, it's unlikely that you'll ever master what you're doing.

Bruce Lee highlights the tremendous benefits of reaching the highest level of focus and concentration. But he also points out that if we can perfect our concentration skills, we can be much more than average.

Successful people I've coached maintain a laser-like focus in life no matter what happens around them.

You've got to concentrate all your thoughts on the work at hand. The sun's rays do not burn until brought to focus.

What's more challenging for most leaders but far more valuable is to fall in love with the problem – like Einstein or Nelson Mandela.

Falling in love with the problem rather than the solution makes it possible to avoid the shiny object syndrome.

There are ways to starve your distractions and feed your focus – one way is to ask yourself three questions simply.

1. What is the most important thing you need to do *right now?*
2. Where are you supposed to be *right now?*
3. *Is this opportunity a distraction, or will it add value to my work?*

DON'T BE A DABBLER – BE A MASTER AT WHAT YOU DO

I encourage you today to avoid the "Shiny Object Syndrome" and commit your life to mastery. Your career will thank you for it. Build the habit of finishing things that you start and achieving the goals that you set for yourself.

Science has proven that whatever you focus on will grow. But we, human beings, are fickle. Our desires are constantly changing. We pursue new things before we finish our old goals. We're dealing with an invisible force that is always trying to confuse us.

Instead of focusing on one thing at a time, we set multiple goals and think we can multitask to achieve them. Yes, you can accomplish a lot of stuff. But just not at the same time. You have to space your goals. You *can* build the career you want, write and publish a book, become a yoga instructor, travel the world, learn how to play the guitar, and speak Italian.

You *can* do all those things but *can't* all at once. And more importantly, you can't excel in any of those fields if you're not willing to invest consistent hours into mastering them. Too often, though, this is the trap we fall into. We spread our energy too thin by going after too many things simultaneously. As a result, we don't end up achieving much. If you want to create sustainable change in your life, you must choose "one thing" and go deep into that thing. And that's the secret to mastery: You do one thing, you do it every day, and you did it for years.

Picasso amassed over 1,800 paintings in his lifetime, but only a fraction was praised and acclaimed. Shakespeare produced 37 plays and 154 sonnets, but only five became famous.

They both produced a lot of work – but they also focused on one single thing:

Picasso painted, and Shakespeare wrote. Bruce Lee's words also exemplify this same principle of mastery: *"I fear not the man who has practiced 10,000 kicks once, but I fear the man who has practiced one kick 10,000 times."*

Mastery and success come from pursuing and doing that one thing for years.

So my question to you is this:

What's your "one thing?"

What's the one thing you want to excel at? What's the one thing you want to focus your energy on? Is it blogging, coding innovation, or stock investing?

Whatever it is, turn off all devices, go in solitude, and give yourself a timeline – one year to write a book, seven months to complete a coding project, and one year to become a director or vice president of the company.

Whatever you choose, you must choose only one. And you must make that "one thing" your priority.

LEADERSHIP CHALLENGE

For the next one month, focus on the most critical task crucial to your success and see how much can be completed without being pulled into another idea.

Power 15

Use Your Million-Dollar Asset

In my coaching career of twenty years, I have done numerous shadow coaching for executives and C.E.O.s of organizations globally. If you don't know what shadow coaching is, it's a part of coaching where I spend two full days with my clients in their work environment, observing how they behave and interact with their team, external stakeholders, and management. I also see their work habits and how they respond in different circumstances. It helps me help them better in bringing about the desired changes.

During shadow coaching, I have seen how some leaders quickly complete a project and transition from one task to another. They make tough decisions with ease and can lead with impact. They can function with ease under stressful circumstances.

How do these leaders perform so well even under pressure?

Some of the world-class leaders whom I've coached, I've taught them to use their million-dollar asset, which is the power of their subconscious mind.

Let me tell you something here: 90% of what you do is done subconsciously. Successful leaders operate well beyond their rational minds. They trust their intuition and gut feelings. Other managers only develop their conscious minds. They assume that's where their power comes from. It comes from their subconscious mind. They will never be more powerful than the mental pictures they have of themselves.

Here's a typical day for my senior leader and C.E.O. clients. Most work 14–16 hours a day, feel perpetually exhausted, and find it difficult to fully engage with their family in the evenings, which leaves them feeling guilty and dissatisfied. Instead of grabbing a bite to eat on the run or working at

DOI: 10.4324/9781003439134-22

their desk, they often sleep poorly, make no time to exercise, and seldom eat healthy meals.

During a coaching session, Sheela shared her frustration at not having the time to get her responsibilities done significantly as her role changed due to the company's exponential growth. Her role now required a shift from operations to strategic thinking and planning, with less focus on maintaining day-to-day operations. She complained that she tried to coach the staff not to come to her for things they could solve themselves, but inevitably, old patterns reemerged. In our coaching session, she asked me to help her figure out how to create new boundaries for herself and her staff.

She expected our conversation to start with questions like, "What tactics have you tried in the past?" But instead, I asked her to brainstorm what emotional rewards (pleasure) she received from being "the hub."

She listed several positives, such as feeling needed, important, and competent. She knew the answers to staff questions and felt safe because her role was critical. Then, we processed the feelings associated with letting go of being "the hub."

She realized she had fears (pain) around her role shifting into areas she wasn't sure she was good at or if she even liked. She shared fears that her role might not be needed as the company changes, and she expressed concern that if she wasn't involved in everything, she might lose control of operations altogether.

This leaves leaders with burnout, which costs both the organization and the employee.

I teach leaders to optimize themselves by managing their energy, not their time. One of the ways is to practice the 5-minute programming technique.

THE 5-MINUTE PROGRAMMING

Here's the difference between people who reach the top and those who do not. And the difference is in their programming. Average people look at programming from outside. They depend on their spouse, teachers, mentors, motivational speakers, and everyone around them. This type of programming is substandard. The world-class wants to take control of their own programming.

One of the things of the world-class is to program themselves for the morning. How do you spend the last 5 minutes of your day? If, like most people, you spend the final 5 minutes of your day complaining of the stress, reading the news, reviewing all the things you don't like, talking and thinking about people you don't get along with and who wronged you, and how terrible your work life is, then you are programming your subconscious mind to marinate on these thoughts in the next 6–8 hours of sleep.

And you wake up the following morning with a heavy head, feel low energy, and go to work feeling irritated. Then you have issues connecting with people and pulling through work, and life seems to create roadblocks in your path and prevent you from succeeding in life or realizing your potential.

So, you want to be extra careful of how you program your subconscious mind. The function of your subconscious mind is to store and retrieve data. Its job is to ensure that you respond precisely to how you are programmed.

All your habits of thinking and acting are stored in your subconscious mind. It has memorized all your comfort zones and works to keep you in them.

What instructions you place into your subconscious mind before you sleep depends on what you do 5 minutes before.

The more in tune with your subconscious you become, the closer you will be to breaking through to success. While most people know the power of a morning routine, there is something just as powerful: an evening routine you can implement every night before you sleep.

As you drift off to sleep, a part of your brain turns off. This process is known as the conscious mind. But while you sleep, a part of your brain is still operating. It operates nonstop: 24 hours a day, 7 days a week, 365 days a year. This is known as your subconscious mind.

Scientists have shown that your subconscious mind is responsible for 95–99% of everything you do daily. Almost every choice you make daily is made not by your conscious mind but by your subconscious programming. It's also 100% more powerful than the conscious mind.

For example, if someone is offered a cigarette, the mind will create two thoughts: Should I smoke or should I not smoke? What are the benefits and the dangers? So, your intellect will give you choices to help you make a better decision. This process will repeat every time someone offers a cigarette. After eight to ten times, the mins automatically stops creating the options in the same situation. It has now gone into your subconscious mind, and you operate in autopilot mode.

Very rarely do we choose if we want to get angry or stay calm in a situation. We automatically get angry if that's what we have consciously chosen in past situations. The mind does not give you options for remaining calm or getting angry. It gets into your subconscious mind.

So, it is imperative for leaders to be aware of their thoughts at the conscious level and choose the proper thoughts so that when they get into the subconscious mind, they are doing the correct things.

Starting tonight and every night for the rest of your life, practice the 5-minute programming technique.

Five minutes before you go off to sleep, begin to program your subconscious mind. Your subconscious mind is relaxed and does deep work when you are asleep. Take an empowering thought and give your subconscious mind to work on it. Repeat that empowering thought when you wake up, and you will start your day in high spirits.

Leaders need no productivity tools and hacks to dictate their day. You need to know how to use the tools you have within you to get you to perform at your best. Great leaders know how to use and program their subconscious minds.

As per another Gallup report – employees who are supervised by highly engaged managers were 59% more likely to be engaged than those supervised by actively disengaged managers. When you are inspired and highly engaged yourself, can you keep your team motivated. And so it's critical that leaders program themselves for success so they can lead the team and the organization towards success.

THE VALUE OF INTUITIVE INSIGHTS

Some of the most successful persons of all time have relied extensively on the intuitive nature of their being. Your success is a true reflection of your internal condition. To change things in your workplace, you must first start by changing things within yourself. Simple as this may appear, however, it is still a very difficult thing to do.

Many years ago, I met a young financial entrepreneur named John. He worked and faced more rejections than he ever expected. Yet, he kept going.

I once asked him what makes him keep moving ahead. With a twinkling in his eyes, he looked at me and replied, "Payal, I have a vision – a goal, if you will. I will one day be a wealthy man. There is a spirit within me that shows me the way to my goal. To hear its voice, I only have to spend some time with myself. In quietness, I find my strength and my answers."

Today, John is a multi-millionaire and owns several highly successful businesses. He credits his success to the art of listening to his inner voice.

This inner voice is within all of us, and it whispers ever so gently. When the noise of everyday problems surrounds us, we tend not to hear the voice.

Within us are all the answers to our problems.

Intuition is a "gift of the gods," so to say. We all were born with it. It is a means of receiving information and guidance through other than the physical senses. One should practice and trust the inner feelings to develop and use this faculty successfully.

As leaders, we need to challenge ourselves to look beyond the surface. This is the perfect time to go deeper and discover what the unconscious motivators are in something that superficially should be easy to solve. Go deep – I guarantee you will discover gems that will aid in change.

LEADERSHIP CHALLENGE

Begin to practice the 5-minute programming technique every day and spend time with yourself alone, listening to your inner voice.

Power 16

Build Your Brand

Do you know what people say about you when you aren't around? It's a question my director asked me during my 1:1 with him when I worked as the senior manager in the organization. The question completely took me off guard.

I had never thought of what people at work were talking about me.

But from that day on, I became conscious of what I wanted to be known for.

Let me ask this to you, "Do you know what you are known for and what you want to be known for?"

Most of us do not consciously think of these questions.

And the more conscious I became of this question, the more I saw that everyone has a brand, whether or not they know it.

For instance, the cashier at the subway was rude toward me because I paid the wrong amount. I believe he had built his brand as an angry young man at work.

Allen, the vice president at a pharmaceutical company, regularly meets and chats with his team worldwide, further developing his warm and friendly personal brand.

The distance between where you are and where you want to be is covered by the brand you build for yourself. Brand is the reputation you create for yourself. It's the story you write for others to talk about you.

In the everyday grinding of our work, we become experts in our field of work. We skill and upskill ourselves; we are trained to give our best each day.

Then suddenly, one day, we find ourselves in the mid-forties and mid-fifties, with our past in the corporate world being more than our future. During this time, it dawns on many that they will soon be out of career life. They begin to feel lost and directionless in their career and soon start to look up books and ask for advice.

DOI: 10.4324/9781003439134-23

As you search for clarity, you try to reach out to some business coaches who tell you to sit back and answer a few questions that will get you where you want to be. And those questions look like this, "*What do I want? Who do I want to become? What do I want my career life to look like in five years? What is my deep purpose?*"

You sit with a paper and pen and begin to think deeply to answer those questions. You feel an "aha'" moment, energized and motivated to conquer the world. You think you are made for something bigger than a nine-to-five job.

All of these feelings have destroyed more careers than shaped them.

Questions like the above are not exactly the right questions to begin with. Why? Because they fall short on two fronts.

First, they assume you know *exactly* what you want, and that's often not the case. Second, they tend to be self-centered and thus neglect to factor in the potential impact we will have on others.

We need to be more intentional and more aligned with our values.

We need a timeless overarching question that we can revert to repeatedly. A question that helps us take our career in the right direction and reflects our core personal values.

I give my clients a two-step exercise that helps them:

1. Step # 1 Ask yourself "What am I known for?"
2. Step #2 Ask others: "What do you think am known for?"

The most interesting part of this exercise is that my clients are surprised to see the difference of perspective between what they think they are known for and what people think they are known for.

The above exercise should be at the core of your leadership. Both these questions help you derive a brand statement for yourself. Before you read ahead, I encourage you to work on this and then write a brand statement for yourself.

THE GREAT ONES CREATE THEIR OWN SELF-IMAGE

Each interaction you have with others has the opportunity to create a memorable experience, teaching them what they can expect from you.

When you're consistent in delivering those experiences, you build a strong brand.

I have coached hundreds and thousands of leaders to develop their uniqueness: your brand – a unique store of value, a distinct and authentic representation of you.

What do you want to be known for? Can you describe it in one word or one sentence?

I remember, when leaving corporate America, I had decided that the one word people could associate with me would be leadership. It's at the core of everything that I do.

How do you want people to think of you?

Are you branding yourself in everything you do and developing and refining your brand?

Here is a simple technique called "Reinventing You" that will help you think through your brand and become aware of the "real" you (Figure P16.1).

- Who am I?
- What's my career purpose?
- What are my values and ethics?
- What's my personality type?
- What is my unique expertise?
- What holds me back?
- What inspires me to move forward?

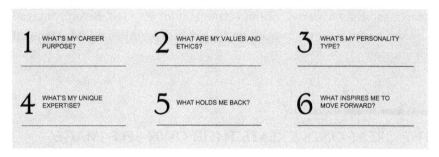

WHO AM I?

1 WHAT'S MY CAREER PURPOSE?	2 WHAT ARE MY VALUES AND ETHICS?	3 WHAT'S MY PERSONALITY TYPE?
4 WHAT'S MY UNIQUE EXPERTISE?	5 WHAT HOLDS ME BACK?	6 WHAT INSPIRES ME TO MOVE FORWARD?

FIGURE P16.1
Reinventing You.

The above questions will help you define who you are as a leader. The brand you create for yourself is the reputation you build with yourself. It affects how people look at you and how they do business with you. It determines the size and scope of the vision you create for yourself. Those who create their self-image for themselves believe almost anything is within their reach. The great ones create their own self-image from scratch by developing a powerful brand statement and working on reinventing themselves with the above questions.

STAND OUT TALL

Distinguishing yourself from others in this noisy corporate world is essential in any industry. Leaders who do not create their brand are constantly pushed from one role to another, and they lose their career direction. Many get off course and give up on their journey toward success.

Don Shula, the legendary NFL football coach who owns the only perfect winning record for an entire NFL season, was asked how he wanted to be remembered, and after a pause, he said, "He played by the rules." He didn't say he was the winningest NFL coach in history (which he is), nor did he mention his perfect season. In other words, to Don Shula, his legacy wasn't about accomplishments. It was about principles. And throughout his career, he kept up with this.

When I was 13, I had an inspiring teacher who one day went right through the class of girls, asking each one, "What do you want to be remembered for?"

None of us, of course, could answer. So she chuckled and said, "I didn't expect you to be able to answer it. But you'll have wasted your life if you still can't answer it by age 40."

How do you want to be remembered as a colleague at work? As a manager or a leader.

Allow the answers to guide your actions and your actions to shape you into who you're becoming.

Whenever you are in a meeting, conference, networking event, or another event, you should be mindful of what others are experiencing and what you want others to share about you.

The best way to live your career life and give it meaning is to live every moment wondering how other people will feel when you leave the corporate world.

In every action you do, think about how your people will remember you: Will they remember you as dependable, calm, trustworthy, someone who made a positive impact, someone who turned around business?

How would you like to be remembered?

Just asking yourself this question thoughtfully and thoroughly can provide direction and purpose to your career journey.

Joseph A. Schumpeter, one of the great economic thinkers of the 20th century, is widely credited with popularizing "creative destruction." Schumpeter posited that innovation is critical to economic dynamism.

So, if you're a leader, think about your employees and how you want them to feel when they work with you. Think about your org and how you want to shape it.

If asked, "How will you be remembered?" What story would you want to be told?

Decide what your story is going to be. You and I both know we have limited time in the corporate world.

THE FINAL GOODBYE NOTE

Like it or not, we'll all come to the end of it, sooner or later. Like I always say, none of us is here forever. We will need to pass the baton to the new workforce.

It reminds me of one of the C.E.O.s I met in California's Silicon Valley. He narrated to me how he always worked with the end in mind. He retired this year-end but had very meticulously prepared for this day. How?

When he stepped into the manager role for the first time, on that very same day, he sat in solitude and wrote down five things he wanted to achieve before he retired.

He reflected on the things that truly mattered: no positions and titles. The only impactful stuff he wanted to do would help him lead a career life of significance and do something impactful at work.

Within a few years, most were done. And in December 2022, he retired with fulfillment.

I believe each of us is here to create history. We are here to do something no one else can do. You are unique. How and for what do you want to be remembered?

Beginning today, I encourage you to take a few pristine hours – hidden away from the world – to generate your list of *5 things you must do before you say your final goodbye from the corporate world.*

I have mine, and I find it helpful to refer to my list. It helps me stay focused on giving the world my best.

LEADERSHIP CHALLENGE

In one clear sentence, write your brand statement, complete the reinventing exercise, and continually ask yourself: How would I like to be remembered?

Power 17

Make Speed Your Best Friend

Do you recollect the airline incident in 2018 where a pilot safely landed a Southwest Airlines passenger plane after a jet engine ripped apart mid-air? The pilot, Shults, had to make a callous decision on an emergency landing. If you hear the audio from the cockpit, which became public, you will notice how calmly Shults spoke with air traffic control. She even surprised herself with her level of calmness as a medic took her vitals after the plane landed. Everyone was amazed at her ability to make such a tough decision with so much precision single-handedly and with speed.

You might not be in a situation like Shults where you must make a life-or-death decision. But every day, you must make decisions at your workplace. Some decisions are relatively simple, while others are critical and tough. Information and training are abundant in decision-making in today's digital world. Yet, in times of crisis and uncertainty, people tend to freeze, they stand still. They say, "I don't know if I want to make a decision." In times like these, we operate with a victim mindset rather than a leadership mindset.

We are in a fast-paced business environment, which is changing quicker than ever. Business decisions have never been more complicated than they are right now. The best leaders can sift through boatloads of information and cut through the complexity to get to the heart of the matter without getting superficial. We are now in a period when leaders are tested continuously against changing conditions and one another.

And so, your speed of action and decision must exceed the speed of events. I've long believed that speed is the ultimate weapon in business. All else being equal, the faster you are, the more you win.

Allan, an exceptional leader whom I coached some years back, would occasionally get a question from his direct reports, "Do you want this done

  DOI: 10.4324/9781003439134-24

fast or right?" His answer was always the same: "Yes, both!" He chose not to compromise on either dimension. For Allan, making mistakes is not an option. But neither is slowing down.

Speed is the combination of doing things fast and doing things right. It's a state of mind that ignites energy and enthusiasm. Speed requires you to reasonably control your emotions, just like the pilot in the earlier incident.

Did you know there are few trees in grasslands to hide animals from predators like lions and tigers? In small grasses, predators can easily locate their prey. So, these animals have to run fast to reach a safe place and escape from their predators. Thus, speed is essential for survival in the grasslands for animals that live there.

Similarly, in business, speed essentially means how quickly your business performs. What is your turnaround time? How soon do you respond to prospect queries, clients' requirements, customer feedback, etc.?

In every company, big or small, the employees are measured by how quickly they get things done. The faster the leader can work on different projects, the more money they are paid. So, what does it mean to be a fast leader? When we talk about speed, we think of leaders who can:

- Spot problems or trends early.
- Quickly respond to problems.
- Quickly make needed changes.

If you are a fast leader, you can get work done efficiently. You can solve any problem that comes your way quickly. Business is all about speed. The faster a company can respond to a customer's needs, the more competitive it will be.

WHAT MAKES A FAST LEADER?

Anyone who has worked with me knows that I am passionate about speed. It's a critical success factor in a competitive world. Of course, speed follows strategy.

For example, the Vasa was a warship built between 1626 and 1628. It is one of the earlier "let's go fast" projects I have read about. The king of

Sweden was in a hurry for various reasons, some of which were important. This project was pushed fast. It was well-funded.

The Vasa sank on its very first time in the water after sailing less than 1 mile, killing 15 people on the ship.

I learned that speed doesn't matter if you crash or sink. I learned that if you crash with the right mindset, you can learn from the crash and increase the speed of the next phase of work.

Basketball, for that matter, is a sport of speed, flexibility, and synchronization. The same qualities are demanded of leaders.

Working with some of the most successful people in the world, I've observed that they follow a straightforward yet powerful equation that helps them speed up.

Speed = Feelings associated with the Event + Clarity of direction

While most of us focus on the event and our actions, successful people consciously focus on the feeling element in speed. They know they cannot control the events in their lives but *can* master *how* they experience them. And that's what differentiates people's results. When people are clear about the direction, speed goes up. When people are not clear, when people don't know who's supposed to be doing what, when people start asking questions like "Where are we going?" then people start going down rabbit holes.

Most people move toward complexity. More to do. More projects. More products. More meetings. More possessions. More goals. And this reduces their speed.

Speed in actions and decision-making isn't so much about skills and knowledge. It's an inner element to be mastered.

Your feelings toward an event and your clarity about what you want will decide the speed of your action.

For instance, when we feel threatened by something, the initial emotion is labeled "fear." That fear produces fight-or-flight responsive feelings, and you slow down in your actions and decisions.

Many say, "When I feel good, I will act." I encourage them to take action to feel good. This is how you can overcome procrastination, too.

It's imperative to be aware of the feeling factor because this area usually has the highest impact on a person's decision.

Deciding to act is not a mindless habit. Every time, it's a conscious effort to achieve higher success rates.

When you have faith in yourself and possess the confidence and self-belief to trust your instincts truly, you're instilled with the ability to make the right decisions without second-guessing your mind. Master your inner leader, and you will master everything around you.

Having now traveled across the globe, meeting people and speaking about leadership at big corporations, I see that people have big career dreams. Some want to start their consultancy firm, some want to get into the C-Suite role, some want to become one of the best leaders, and others want to change their industry.

However, most of these leaders lack speed because they fear taking action and making decisions with speed. It seems overwhelming when they think of the "how."

Many of us face this problem. We want to do something, but we procrastinate and slow down. You feel your current reality doesn't seem to match your dream. And everything seems impossible. I don't know your goals, but I want you to know that the word "how" is a dream killer. I have experienced this state very closely in my journey.

Let me tell you something I have learned while associating with one of the C.E.O.s of a manufacturing firm in Japan. While talking to him about my dream to do something big for corporates in India, I told him about my confusion on the "how" part. He said:

> Payal, how is none of your business. That is the work of the higher power, the universe, whatever name you call it. Very often, we get overwhelmed while deciding on our dreams. Your business is to stick closely like a super-glue to your dream, to pick yourself up after every fall and failure, to work on yourself consistently, and to know your why. The solution to not getting overwhelmed by the how is to not think of all the moves ahead of time. Just plan the best-possible next move, then plan the next one from that space. It's always about just the next step, Payal, only the next best step. You will soon enjoyably reach your destination.

Her words still ring in my ears – even today, when I get overwhelmed by how I think of just the next best step.

When you think of the next best step, you pick up speed in your decision and action.

The speed at which leaders work makes a huge difference. People love leaders who can act with speed and act right.

One of the questions I often get asked is if leaders can increase their speed without burning out. And the answer is an absolute yes.

Burnout happens when we begin ordering everybody to move faster. Burnout occurs when we say yes to everything and everyone and take up more than we can consume. It happens when you begin to manage by fear or manage by crisis.

When you work with a sense of urgency every day, having a realistic view of time, means acting now for a result that will be realized five years later. This avoids burnout.

I was once doing shadow coaching for Kim, the head of a company providing an AI-based platform for robotic process automation at Milpitas, San Jose. In one of the meetings about a production issue in Japan, Kim remarked to her production head, John, "This is bad. Someone ought to get over there and get this resolved." Thirty minutes passed, and suddenly Kim looked back at John and asked, "Why are you still here?" John left the meeting immediately, drove directly to San Francisco Airport, and got on the next flight to Japan without even a change of clothes. But you can bet that the problem was resolved fast.

I can positively affirm that with every increasing year, everything is moving faster. Speed is your best friend while making it to the top. Speed is often the only thing that makes the difference between winning and losing. It's not that everything needs to be done *now*, but it's always helpful to challenge the due date for items on your critical path. All it takes is asking the most straightforward question: "Why can't this be done sooner?"

It's no secret that the pace of change in business today is unprecedented. Leaders who act quickly and inspire others to do the same are the ones who ultimately win each day and reach the top.

LEADERSHIP CHALLENGE

Be conscious of your feelings associated with the event, and take action to feel good.

Power 18

Optimize Your Weekends

This is one of the simplest powers to practice, yet most of us find it the toughest. But to attain high success, you must be willing to work. We all want to make it to the top and believe that working 70 hours a week will do it for us. But here's a crazy fact: a 2014 study from Stanford called "The Productivity of Working Hours" reveals that productivity per hour declines sharply when you work more than 50 hours.

And so, more than ever, it's crucial to nail the weekend. Come Monday, it's so easy to feel guilty, asking yourself the same weekly questions: Where did the time go? Why didn't I make the most of it? Why don't I feel like I've had a weekend?

Why do you think most people aren't able to reach great heights in their careers?

Take, for example, Ray, a 46-year-old C.M.O. of a startup company. His day starts at 10.00 am and ends at around 8.00 pm, Monday to Friday. Come Friday, he will spend time with friends over a beer. Over the weekend, Ray would usually wake up late, laze around, catch up on the news, and spend his day on the couch. At night, he would often catch up with friends again or watch web series.

I met Ray at the Thanksgiving dinner gala organized by one of my client companies. Ray dreams of quitting his day job and starting his marketing consultancy by age 50. But he hasn't started doing any work toward it.

You see, my friend, like Ray, you too won't get there by sitting still, making plans, and dreaming about how awesome it will be once you achieve your mission. Instead, you've got to make it a daily, hourly habit to do the work it takes to move forward, no matter how difficult it is.

The most significant difference between average and peak performers lies in their weekends. These world-class performers don't have superpowers.

DOI: 10.4324/9781003439134-25

The rules they've crafted for themselves allow bending of reality to such an extent that it might seem that way, but they've learned how to optimize their weekends, and so can you.

More than 80% of these successful leaders have some form of weekend practice.

These are messy times. Days of intense volatility. A period of immense uncertainty. To be a peak performer, deliver the best results, rise above the crowd, and be visible at your work and business, you've got to do what peak performers do. If you want to achieve the results only 5% reach, you've got to think, produce, and behave like only 5% of the people on the planet; then here's what your mantra should be.

Just before the Christmas weekend of 2015, I spoke at a huge tech conference in Montreal. On my flight home, I sat near one of America's top financial gurus. I couldn't hold myself back and began a conversation with him. Now, one of the questions I ask most super-successful people I meet is about their weekends.

I was blown away by listening to how this financial guru optimizes his weekends. He said he spends his weekend thinking. Sometimes, he analyzes his business strategies. Other times, he is dreaming of new projects. Still, some other times, he's being introspective. At times, he is reading about life and health.

It made me think deeply about the fact that the difference between average and peak performers lies in their weekend routines. One of the most significant habits of peak performers is how productive they make their weekends.

Making time to think is a superb strategy for success. Most of us are so busy doing that we don't know where to go. Suddenly, layoffs hit us, our contracts expire, we get passed over for a promotion, and we realize that we never had time to work on ourselves. We were just busy doing, not being who we could be.

So, while many people see the weekend as a time to hang out and relax, exceptionally successful people have a different idea of how Saturdays and Sundays should be spent. Here is how *they* spend their weekends to set the tone for a week of crazy, productive work.

Here are five habits to help you have the most productive weekend so that you are more than ready not just for Monday but also to achieve your career aspiration. These weekend habits will work incredibly and make an immediate difference in your life, helping you become an excellent leader.

HABIT #1: HAVE A PLAN

Weekdays go by quickly in completing your targets, team meetings, and planning. But what about your weekends? Do you have a plan for every weekend? Apart from relaxing and family time, what about a plan for your self-development? If you want to achieve more, it won't happen purely because of your hardwork during your working hours. Your weekends need to be enriched.

HABIT # 2: PRACTICE STILLNESS

I coach and speak to thousands of high-end executives globally. And what I often hear is that there is no time to sit and practice stillness. A leader's power comes from self-awareness that is responsive to feedback but independent of the good or bad opinions of others. Use your weekend for sitting in stillness and calming down your running mind.

HABIT # 3 REFLECT

The best way to move ahead and be 110% ready for Monday with total momentum is to reflect on the week gone by. Most people do this instead of taking the time to analyze their week's experience; they move on to the next one, never learning from their mistakes. We have all heard the phrase "experience is the best teacher" a million times. We can't learn from experience if we don't take the time to reflect on what message it is trying to give us. Actively think about what it is you are trying to improve. Ask yourself the following questions: "What do I want?" "Why do I want it?" "What are my goals?" "Do I need to change any of my goals?"

HABIT # 4: STRENGTHEN YOUR INSTINCTS

Leaders and entrepreneurs must make many decisions in their daily work lives. If you cannot trust your experiences and instincts, you will most likely depend on others around you for suggestions. We all have this innate ability to listen to that inner voice telling us not to go through with something or to go ahead and take a risk. But in the daily grinding of the work, our instincts weaken. Use time over the weekend to strengthen and apply this during the week.

HABIT # 5: READ

I save articles throughout the day to a folder called "Read It," and then I spend an hour or two on the weekend absorbing the new ideas.

SUCCESS IS NOT AN ACCIDENT

"Weekend? Wow! I can at least relax after a week's hectic workload!" This is a common phrase said by most people. Success demands you work on weekends. Now, the type of work is essential. If, over the weekend, you are doing precisely the same work you do from Monday to Friday, it's no good.

Now, don't get me wrong. If there is a deadline looming or a massive project or customer deadline, then working late nights, early mornings, and weekends might be the only way to get it done. Been there, done that. But never accept it as usual.

Optimizing your weekends is not about being busy. The busier you are, the worse you are at time management.

How you spend your time says everything about what you value. As a leader, you must be clear on your priorities. My priorities are my family and work. Personally, I believe work–life balance is a myth. I don't switch on and off between work; it just happens naturally.

What you do off the job significantly affects how far you go on the job. How many good books do you read each year? How often do you attend workshops? Who do you spend most of your time with?

Early on, when I entered the field of coaching and speaking, I had to knock on many corporate doors to get entry. I do not ever remember looking forward to knocking on that first door. I finally took the advice of one of my early mentors, who suggested I make an appointment with myself to reach out to my prospects at precisely the same time each day. He then suggested I put it off my mind until it was time for that appointment. This approach helped me tremendously in the early years of my coaching practice, and I was able to eliminate procrastination and worry.

We have undoubtedly said, "I don't feel like it," several times. Do it, and you will feel like doing it.

So, while many people see the weekend as a time to hang out and relax, exceptionally successful people have a different idea of how Saturdays and Sundays should be spent. In one of the episodes of my podcast, *The Payal Nanjiani Leadership Podcast*, I speak about how *successful leaders* spend their weekends setting the tone for a week of crazy productive work.

A C.E.O. once told me that what happens between Friday night and Monday morning determines your success level. There are a lot of books, articles, and blog posts out there about the weekday habits of successful people. Things like waking up early, eating a healthy breakfast, and unplugging at the end of the day tend to get included in these lists. But what happens between Friday night and Monday morning? That's where the game changes for a few.

If the world's best are stretching themselves to get strong, why aren't you? When you optimize your weekends, you'll find that every measure of performance skyrockets exponentially. Doors you knew that never existed will begin to open.

Why be average when you and I know you are built to be achievers?

LEADERSHIP CHALLENGE

Make a plan for self-development every weekend.

Power 19

Take Your People with You

Teamwork is such an overused and clichéd topic. So, what does it mean to work in a team? How can you capitalize on the strength of your team to add magic and that "zing" to your projects?

Here is a story that beautifully illustrates this idea and provides a little practical understanding of the concept.

Once, while walking in the forest, a little girl spotted a large log on the ground. Curious, she asked her father if she could move it.

Her father replied, "Yes, you can. Use all your strength." Excited by the challenge, the little girl tried to move the log with all her might, failing to do so. Not wanting to let down her father's faith in her, she tried repeatedly. But she couldn't move the log.

Frustrated, she turned to her father and said, "You lied to me. You said I could move the log, but I can't." The father asked her, "Did you use all your strength?" The little girl said, "Yes, I did. I used all my strength; you saw me struggle, get hurt, and give up." The father replied, "No, you did not use all your strength. I stood right here the whole time, but you didn't use me to move the log. My presence in your life is your strength. Why would you not use me when you need it?"

In conclusion, the little girl's story reminds us to use all our strength to achieve our goals. We have unique strengths, but sometimes, that may not be enough to complete the job. As a habit, we must also tap into the strengths of others – it is a great empowerment tool to learn, grow, and become better.

However, most of us prefer to work in isolation. We hire the best team members, but refuse to delegate work to them. We underutilize the potential of our team. We underestimate the power of our team members. We micromanage them and lack trust in our own people.

 DOI: 10.4324/9781003439134-26

My client, Taylor, is an EVP with more than seventeen years of experience with a large retail chain. She has worked with some of the top companies in the world and is extremely well-connected. But her boss, Jack, doesn't see Taylor's value and does not promote her. In all likelihood, I think Taylor threatens Jack. And so, Taylor had no other option but to resign and join another company.

Many leaders like Jack fail to utilize the power of their people. They feel threatened by their team members' achievements and potential.

Do you know what "Rolling Swarm" is?

It's a group of caterpillars, moving in a formation wherein "swarm" of caterpillars moves faster than any single caterpillar. That's the power of unity. Alone we can do so little; together we can do so much, said Helen Keller.

To reach the top, you must support your people, sponsor them, and mentor them. They are not threatened by them but instead use their talents to make the team, the function, and the entire organization better.

True leaders know they don't lose power by empowering their direct reports. They gain more influence and become the leaders everyone else wants to work with and for.

I often tell my clients that they must consciously be grateful for their team before they start their workday. Without the team, there is no leader. There is no success.

One of the questions I ask leaders during my team coaching program is, "What is the main duty of a leader?" Most people say that the primary duty of any leader is to achieve the results. Well, that's partially correct. The fundamental duty of a leader is not to get the results. In reality, a leader is never directly responsible for the result.

The fundamental duty of a leader is to empower their people to get the results – however, insecurity factors heavily in the downfall of some of the best leaders. Rather than empowering others, they clutch at power so tightly that they lose all sense of morality and ethics.

So why do so many people in management positions fail to empower their subordinates? The reason is that many of us operate with a feeling of insecurity.

Today, we have many insecure leaders in the corporate world. And you can see their insecurity in many ways. Insecure leaders:

- Want to be liked and praised.
- Adore positions and titles.

- Try to hold on to information so they are seen as the smartest in the room.
- Are afraid to share their knowledge and experience.
- Won't ask for advice.
- Don't like feedback.
- Micromanage people and business.
- Avoid confrontation.
- Takes credit for the team's achievements.
- Lack of self-worth.

When I coach insecure leaders, they often remind me of a scene in Star Wars IV. Princess Leia Organa speaks with General Tarkin, telling him, "The more you tighten your grip, Tarkin, the more star systems will slip through your fingers."

If you genuinely want to grow at your work and be successful, you must be led with a sense of security. You must lead with a feeling of security.

The most outstanding leaders are those who are secure. They are the ones who:

- Share information.
- Share their knowledge.
- Experience so that others will benefit.
- They are never afraid that someone else might go ahead of them.
- Have courage.
- Delegate effectively.
- Give power to others to make decisions.
- Believe in their team.
- Love to give others credit.
- Work on upgrading and empowering themselves.

It is such leaders whom I have seen achieve the highest level of success in their profession. They have a strong sense of self-worth.

One of the most outstanding leaders of the United States, Abraham Lincoln, was known for his willingness to give his power and authority. Lincoln brilliantly assembled a cabinet from his Republican opponents to preserve the Union and win the Civil War. None of these men had high regard for Lincoln. But, Lincoln did not want a group of "yes" men to agree with his every decision. He wanted a cabinet of passionate advisors who could shed light on the country's complex issues, were free to question his authority, and were unafraid to argue with him.

A team is created with strong and able individuals coming together for a larger purpose, one that they will accomplish "together." So relying on and capitalizing on each other's strengths is not just intelligent but also the right thing to do. That is why you have been put in a team – to work together on each other's points of power. You wouldn't be called into an organization if you were meant to work alone.

The call for power intervention is sometimes in the frame of asking for help – do it. It doesn't make you small, but it can save the project. Often, we need to ask for help, rely on others, or tap into different resources to make something happen. It is suitable for you and good for the project at hand.

You can't make it to the top if you are not secure. When employees feel supported by their bosses, they are more secure and confident in their work. The results of such feelings are increases in morale and attitude.

To grow as a leader, you must learn to give power away – empower others to take on new responsibilities. This, in turn, frees you to grow in new areas. Always remember that empowering others empowers you.

LEADERSHIP CHALLENGE

Pick one quality of a secure leader and lead with a sense of security.

Power 20

Play Politics, but Come Out Clean

Have you ever said to yourself, "I will never play corporate politics," or "I just prefer to stay away from corporate politics?" I often hear these kinds of statements during my 1:1 coaching with some senior leaders. I make it a point to ask my clients, "How good are you at corporate politics?" And most of them shy away from politics.

Office politics can be a complex topic for many people. In my corporate workshops, I always ask the participants to tell me what comes to their mind when they think of the word office politics. Ninety-nine percent of the words given are negative. "Toxic," "frustrating," "dangerous," "demotivating," "draining," "unfair," "unnecessary," "cliques," and "gossip" almost always rise to the surface.

Politics is inevitable in the workplace. All workplaces are political to some extent.

You've got to accept that everyone has their agenda and personal ambitions when they enter the workforce. People bring their personal emotions, needs, ambitions, and insecurities in their professional lives.

We all want to be successful, and often, these ambitions and emotions don't align with everyone else's because, in essence, different elements are competing for limited resources. This is bound to lead to uncomfortable political climates.

Rachna worked as an executive across the nonprofit sector for over two decades. Throughout these years, she refused to engage in office politics as a badge of honor. She believed politics was dreadful, dangerous, and unnecessary. She thought that she was here for her work, and that's it.

However, she was entirely unprepared and out of her depth when she was laid off several years into her career. It wasn't because she performed poorly or failed to meet her goals. It was because she had neglected to form

DOI: 10.4324/9781003439134-27

relationships with people with power and refused to be in the office's inner circles of politically well-connected people.

The experience made her realize it was high time she became more *politically* intelligent at work.

WORKING HARD WILL NOT BE ENOUGH

Many of us believe that working hard will do it all for us. And so Our most common mistake is not having a realistic understanding of what makes some people more successful than others. I've observed so many people kill themselves at their jobs, working late and on weekends, happy hour networking, staying in close proximity to the boss, taking up more work and sacrificing themselves and their aspirations at the cost of their families.

In the organization, hard work does not move you much from where you are to where you want to be. You need to analyze your game and play it differently now, on or else someone else around you will be more than happy to leverage your weakness. At every level you have to play the game better to win.

Politics is inescapable, from NGOs to churches to startups to Fortune 500 companies.

Corporate politics is a force that can be used and harnessed for individual gain and the benefit of the organization and society.

To make it to the top, you must know how to play politics and come out clean.

Though you might reach some level of success by working hard, there are many opportunities you will miss due to your lack of education about office politics. It's not a subject covered in most colleges or business schools, even though it's essential to surviving (and thriving) in every work environment.

In my work as a global coach, that's why I've prioritized educating professionals at every stage in their careers on organizational politics and how to navigate them at work.

You must be aware of what's happening around you; you must be able to be a part of inner groups and work well alongside the group.

Watching the difference in people's reactions is fascinating, as some individuals can find good in anything, a silver lining in every cloud.

In my twenty-one years of coaching and training leaders, I've often been asked why some people are better at navigating politics than others. Here's why and how great leaders navigate corporate politics and come out clean.

For example, let's say you have a big meeting coming up where stakeholders at your company decide which projects to invest in. If you're savvy at politics, you know that to get your project approved, you first need to understand the priorities and perspectives of those stakeholders. You need to engage with and influence them by learning what they seek.

This is an example of how office politics can be ethically used to help you gain an advantage. You play politics, but come out clean.

Even so, destructive and harmful politics can – and do – exist. In the same situation, if you were to spread a rumor behind your colleague's project to get yours chosen over hers, that would be an unethical use of politics.

Playing politics at work can be done in ways where you do not dirty your hands. This can be done by building alliances where you'll support the other person's career needs in return for that person's support in satisfying your career needs. You can do favors and take favors in return. However, you will, whatever the case, never let corporate politics drain you and consume you.

Dealing with office politics can be stressful, especially if you feel like a target. However, it's possible to survive office politics if you constantly stay professional. If you're already the target of office politics, you can deal with the bad behavior of others without losing your reputation.

Let me share a fable with you that will help you deal well with politics in the workplace.

Once, a donkey a farmer owned fell into a well. The donkey cried miserably for hours as the farmer tried to figure out what to do. Finally, the farmer thought that as the donkey was old and the well needed to be covered anyway, it wasn't worth saving the donkey. So he invited all his neighbors to come over and help him.

They all grabbed a shovel and began to shovel dirt into the well. At first, the donkey realized what was happening and cried horribly. Then, to everyone's amazement, the donkey quietened down. A few shovelloads later, the farmer finally looked down the well and was astonished at what he saw. The donkey did something unusual with every scoop of dirt that hit his back. He would shake it off and take a step up. As the farmer's neighbors continued shoveling dirt on top of the animal, he would shake it off and step up. Pretty soon, everyone was amazed as the donkey stepped up over the edge of the well and trotted off!

Workplace politics is just the same. In your work life, too, plenty of people will shovel dirt on you, all kinds of trash – through their actions, words, or behaviors. They aim to disturb you because if you allow their words and actions to stick to you then you are going to feel bad – there's going to be pain, and you will also start reacting, and then you will go on a downward spiral. And this is what they wanted; they wanted you out of their way, and you cleared the path for them.

But the trick to achieving success when surrounded by corporate politics or negativity is to shake it off and step up. You've got to remain neutral during praise and criticism. By doing so, you are permitting yourself to focus *only* on the following action that takes you toward your vision.

Being in this state helps you make the best decisions in the most challenging moments.

If you remember to shake it off and step up, nothing will disturb you, and you will be an unstoppable leader.

You've got to remember that people play politics with you only when they know you are doing a great job. Your greatness hurts them. So, your job is to continue working on your greatness.

How you respond to the dirt thrown on you will determine your actions. Always keep track of the politics but don't get sucked up playing it. There are many smart ways to navigate.

Corporate politics is not about knowing how to put others down. It's an art of knowing on how to put others up. When was the last time you asked your boss about his journey? When did you ask your chairman on what he sees in any team? When did you speak positvely about the person next to you in the board meeting?

I remember in one of my recent workshops for female leaders, I told them the importance of learning how to feed someone's ego. And immediately they all resented this thought as buttering. Feeding someone's ego is not about buttering, its about making someone feel valuable. Think about it. Don't you feel elated and happy when someone asks you for some advice or tells you that you are brilliant at something. Well, it feeds your ego.

If you know how to feed someone's ego positively and put others up, you will navigate corporate politics like sailing in a smooth sea. And best of all, you will come out clean.

LEADERSHIP CHALLENGE

Practice shaking it and stepping up.

Power 21

Cut the Cord at the Right Time

Ray was a successful PR head at a start-up company in Arizona. Ray loved his job; he loved everything about his career. He would go more than an extra mile to take up projects in various roles. At one point, when the company was facing a cash crisis, Ray worked more for the company to help it come out of the situation. The company's founder verbally promised Ray higher monetary benefits during that time. Ray worked harder for the company and always felt for the company as if it was his baby.

In 2018, the company's founder was booked for fraudulent activities. The case went on for a year. Many of its prominent board of directors stepped down. Massive layoffs occurred, and people weren't paid their dues as the company filed for bankruptcy.

Ray, too, lost all of his verbally promised benefits and salary, which amounted to almost five million dollars.

Ray was emotionally attached to his work. He was so attached that he did not realize the company was failing and would soon lose his job. And on December 24th, just before Christmas, Ray was politely asked to leave as the company was downsizing big time.

This incident broke Ray from the inside. How could a company for which he gave his life do this to him? This question kept disturbing Ray. It took him months to get out of this zone and into another job.

Ray could've saved himself from getting into this zone had he known how to cut the cord with the company.

Many leaders get too emotionally attached to their jobs, titles, teams, and projects. The attachment to their work blinds them, and they detach from everything else around them.

My client Lui loved her job. Her assignments were interesting across various verticals, and she was paid exceptionally well. The only problem

DOI: 10.4324/9781003439134-28

was that Lui would get highly emotionally invested in her work, impacting her personal life and clouding her judgments at work. Once, her boss called a last-minute meeting on a Friday afternoon to discuss an upcoming project. Even though the late project was beyond Lui's control, she felt that correcting the timeline landed solely on his shoulders. Lui worked all weekend to get the initiative back on track, sacrificing her twenty-fifth wedding anniversary.

Many high-achievers can relate to Lui, and Ray's was out of Lui's portfolio of work; she took it up and believed it was on her to make the company a success. This further impacted her family life.

Being emotionally invested in your work is like a double-edged sword. Your drive and passion propel you to perform at the cost of your health, time, and family.

But being *too* emotionally tied to your job can become a huge drain and weight to carry. While there's typically nothing wrong with devoting yourself to your organization's success, problems arise when work controls your feelings and actions.

I want you to reflect on a few of these questions: Is your job more than a means to an end? Has it become your identity? Is it giving you a feeling of security? Does your work define you as an individual? It's easy to see why we can often take things too personally, try to overcompensate, or become too attached to an arbitrary outcome. It's because we become too emotionally invested in our jobs.

So, how can you tell if you're too emotionally invested in your work? Look for these signs that it's time to pull back:

1. Work follows you home.
2. Your identity is your job title.
3. You take things too personally at work.
4. You try to prove your importance.
5. You internalize criticism.
6. You obsessively check work messages and emails.

I have seen leaders who became very attached to their jobs. When those jobs ended – as all jobs eventually do – these leaders invariably suffered depression. A few never recovered.

A job isn't your identity. A job isn't your reason for being. You are much more. Your importance and worth transcend any single job.

Caring deeply about your performance provides satisfaction and meaning. But being too emotionally tied to your job can become a huge drain and weight to carry. While some emotional attachment to your work can give you a sense of belonging, stability, and happiness, becoming too emotionally attached can impede your growth and consume your identity.

One of the greatest icons of India, the brilliant missile man of India, Dr APJ Abdul Kalam, is famously quoted as follows:

"Love your job, but don't love your company, as you never know when the Company stops loving you."

These words mean a lot to any employee who wants mental well-being. Emotional attachment to your job may sound positive, but it's unhealthy in the long run.

1. Nobody, including you, is irreplaceable in a corporate scenario.
2. It's easier to manipulate a worker who is emotionally invested in the job than someone who is not. Manipulations could range from stalling promotions to making promises or offers for never-fulfilled raises.
3. When you are too attached to your job, dealing with criticism is difficult.
4. Getting a worker emotionally attached to the work environment is a surefire way to make him work for less money.
5. In the event of downsizing for any reason, it will be tough for an employee who is too emotionally attached to his job.
6. When you are too attached to the work, you find ways to rationalize whatever negativities at work, even when it hampers your personal growth.
7. Too much emotional attachment to work could affect work–life balance.

This does not mean you shouldn't give your best at work. It means you must be aware of your attachment type.

There are two types of work attachment:

1. Secure attachment

The secure attachment style refers to forming secure, loving relationships with your work. Someone with this style can trust others and be trusted.

Those with a secure attachment style at work take tasks as they come, do their best, and leave the rest. They work hard and do not fear saying no when they need to. They know they are capable and confident and do not require validation. If you have a secure attachment style at work, you will likely manage your time well and achieve an excellent work–life balance.

2. Anxious attachment

This type of attachment at work is the type of insecure attachment. They feel everything at work is their responsibility. They have a fear of upsetting others. They want to control everything and feel it's up to them to complete every task. It can impede your growth, consume your identity, and convince you that your dedication protects you from change or adversity. This type of attachment is dangerous because it blinds you, just like it blinded Rehan.

Some years back, I was working in a software company. There was another employee, Rehan, who was senior to me. He was the company's first employee who had joined at its inception. Now, he joined this company because he was emotionally attached to the company's boss. In the initial years, he often worked without a salary, too, because the company had financial problems, but later, financial problems were solved, and the company started doing very well.

Rehan was very hard-working and fully committed. He did not try to search for a job elsewhere. Even the owner of the company often said that Rehan was like family.

Then, the company started putting the owner's close relatives and friends in senior positions. These employees did not have any knowledge and were very arrogant. But, they were unduly favored.

A day came when the company decided to get funds from a venture capitalist. The venture capitalist decided to put its people in senior positions. Rehan was asked to leave the company. He did not have another job at that time. He hadn't even prepared his resume.

When you become emotionally attached to a company, you become blindfolded and let many great opportunities pass.

A job isn't your identity. A job isn't your reason for being. You are much more. Your importance and worth transcend any single job.

The more attachment we develop to our job, the more difficult it becomes to break.

I found myself so weak when I had to leave the job or the company which I got used to. When I started believing and following that we should not love the company but should love the position we take up, I felt less emotional at the workplace and happier and stress free.

For many, a job is more than a means to an end; it is an identity. It gives us a feeling of security, defines us as individuals, and offers us purpose. It's easy to see why we can often take things too personally, try to overcompensate, or become too attached to an arbitrary outcome.

The boss had a bad morning at the Q2 budget meeting. A coworker is stressed and seems short. There was an error in the last memo that went out, and someone should have caught it but didn't, and now a supervisor is mad.

People who are attached to their jobs are the ones who tend to take things too personally at work.

My cord of attachment at work is so strong that it kills your sound judgment. *Many of us have a work-first mentality, but is it pervading your personal life too?*

We must gain awareness of what we truly want and need out of our work lives, not to mention what would make us happy and fulfilled. Take the time to define what success and happiness at work mean to you so that you can start taking intentional action toward that vision.

Once you have clarity on your work happiness vision, you'll need to clarify your nonnegotiables and priorities to protect them with boundaries.

LEADERSHIP CHALLENGE

Be conscious to check if you have a secure or anxious attachment at your workplace.

Power 22

Build Emotion Strength

In 2014, I learned one of my life's most important lessons, which was to develop a high degree of emotional strength. Because of this critical lesson, I stayed longer in the game and built a name for myself compared to other women of color from India in the coaching and book-writing industry in America.

I learned this valuable lesson while attending a conference where one of the military commandos was the speaker. He talked about the Beast Barracks.

Approximately 1,300 cadets join the entering class at the United States Military Academy, West Point, each year. During their first summer on campus, cadets are required to complete a series of brutal tests. This summer initiation program is known internally as "Beast Barracks."

"Beast Barracks is deliberately engineered to test the limits of cadets' physical, emotional, and mental capacities."

Interestingly, it wasn't strength, smarts, or leadership potential that accurately predicted whether or not a cadet would finish Beast Barracks. Instead, their emotional strength predicted whether or not a cadet would be successful, not their talent, intelligence, or genetics.

That evening, when I left the conference, I decided to work harder on my emotional strength than my skills and abilities. It is this emotional strength that helped me make better decisions and stay through it all.

The Bible teaches us that our thoughts are the determining factor that controls our actions. Bhagavad Gita says the mind is undoubtedly restless and difficult to curb, but it can be controlled by repeated practice and detachment.

We cannot change our actions without changing our emotions. It's not just what we think about that needs changing; we must change our thinking process. Our emotions are linked directly to how we feel.

DOI: 10.4324/9781003439134-29

Anger, frustration, depression, jealousy, and insecurity. They are killing us every day. They are taking away our happiness and pushing us into a vicious cycle where we encounter regret at each end.

But sadly, it seems we just can never get over it. We start with anger and end with regret. And this continues again and again until one day we realize that work life has become something more of "surviving" than "winning and thriving."

Sapna had put in hours of work on a presentation. She was excited about the presentation she'd give to her company's senior leaders and stakeholders soon. If her presentation went well, it could mean a promotion for her in the next quarter. She rehearsed her slides, and her colleague pointed out a flaw in her presentation strategy as she came closer to the presentation day. It completely threw Sapna off as she thought of the weeks of hardwork she'd put into preparing for this.

In a rage, she threw the whole presentation away and called out sick to avoid further discussions. In her absence, the management had to cancel the meeting, which cost the company their contract. Sapna's performance and commitment to her work were questioned, and she regrets her decision, which she made purely out of anxiety and anger.

Many of us behave like Sapna. We blow up things rather than thinking through the problem and working on it.

How easy would it have been for Sapna to add an additional slide or edit the pre-existing slides with the concerns shared by her colleague?

She could use it as a jumping-off point to open the conversation for questions and feedback. The leaders would have been impressed with her hardwork, authenticity, and foresight.

To reach the top, you must build emotional strength to push past your insecurities and find the silver lining.

As Thomas Edison said, *"I have not failed. I've just found 10,000 ways that won't work."* He could say this because he did not let the emotions of failure overpower him.

Most of us don't get to the top because we blame our circumstances. We equate our mindset with the situation. If the problem is tough or rough, our emotions of worry, anxiety, and stress take over, and then we make irrational decisions. If the situation is favorable, we get excited and make some irrational choices again.

Now let me ask you something I ask in my corporate workshops: Do you think a situation and our mindset are connected? Most of the responses I get are yes; situations and our state of mind are deeply connected. As the problem, so is our state of mind, say many.

Now think of the number of people you know who have everything in life but are not happy. They complain and make a mountain of every small problem. You look at them, question how someone can have everything, and always complain. These people are proof that our state of mind has nothing to do with the situation.

I want you to take a deep breath, pause, and rank yourself on a scale of 1–10 on emotional strength. How often is your state of mind dependent on the situation and people's behavior?

So why do some people accomplish their goals while others fail? What makes the difference?

Usually, we answer these questions by talking about these people's talent, strategy, or skills. But we all know there is more to the story than that.

What makes a bigger impact than talent or intelligence? Emotional strength.

Research is starting to reveal that your emotional strength is more important than anything else for achieving your goals in health, business, and life.

Emotional strength is a quality of mind where the mind refuses to be intimidated and can control emotions and remain highly focused when under the pressure of intense competition; that is, the ability to identify and manage your own emotions and the emotions of others.

One of the senior directors I coached a couple of years back was a subject-matter expert. He was thorough in being proactive and knew how to achieve results at all costs.

What made him a bad leader? He was overly critical of himself and of the people he supervised. He was not a good sender or receiver of communication. One of the emotions he always struggled with was anger and frustration. Over time, his anger and frustrations would get the better of him in complex workplaces, and he'd gradually become more annoyed and less able to control his emotions.

Knowing how to ride those peaks and valleys allows people to reach the top and build momentum in their companies to prepare for all the loops, twists, and turns.

Often, when leaders are experiencing emotional highs and lows, they make these three critical mistakes:

- *We say things off the cuff.*
- *We make decisions we wish we didn't.*
- *We damage those who work directly with us.*

Emotional strength is a personality trait that determines your ability to perform consistently under stress and pressure.

LEARN TO MANAGE YOUR EMOTIONS

A leader not managing their emotions well can wreak severe havoc on an organization, seriously damaging employee morale, retention, and, ultimately, the bottom line. Every reaction – positive or negative – will have consequences for all those under them and affect the company's overall success.

Emotional control is a skill that most leaders need to be successful in managing their employees. Therefore, leaders need to prepare to present a calm, rational front. When leaders have high emotional control, they are seen as likable and ethical and work in the organization's interest.

To be in control of one's emotions means maintaining personal composure during times of stress, when things are uncertain, or when faced with conflict or disagreement. This does not mean suppressing all emotions but instead consciously choosing which emotions are appropriate and avoiding expressing extreme or negative emotions under pressure.

My father always taught me to be neutral in both "happiness and sadness." It is obvious that it is not easy for a person to do that, but this is possible with meditation. Don't be too happy and don't be too sad because excess of everything is bad.

I read this story somewhere. Once, a frustrated rich man went to a sage and told him all his problems.

He said, "I am not feeling well these days. I just cannot control my anger. My head and stomach ache the whole day, and I always feel sleepy. My brother and wife fight with me whenever I talk to them, and my servants don't like me."

The sage said, "I don't have a solution to your problems." After many requests, the sage told him, "He will die after ten days."

This left the man aghast. He asked the sage for the solution.

The sage replied, "Death is certain, and no one can avert it." He thanked the sage and left.

On the ninth day, he returned and apologized for not giving the sage anything that day.

The sage asked, "How did your nine days go?"

The man said, "Everyone treated me nicely. Surprisingly, I didn't feel angry and lived every single minute. My wife and my brother love me so much. It was me who always talked angrily with them."

The sage replied, "You found the solution to your problem. When you learned that you had only ten days to live, you didn't waste it getting angry over small things."

The "Then Frustrated, now Happy" man understood, gave the sage some money, and left.

Anger and frustration are two major emotion waves leaders ride on.

In chapter 2 of The Bhagavad Gita, Lord Krishna says, "Death is Certain." "Any day can be our last day."

Most of us know that anger affects our thinking and makes our thoughts rigid. If we see the cause and effect of anger, we can control it. So, pen down all the things that make you angry and stop doing them.

You have the power to change anything because you are the one who chooses your thoughts, and you are the one who feels your emotions.

If you control your emotions, you'll control your day. By understanding the root causes and effects of any problem, we can easily navigate to the solution. Every solution lies in the problem. In this way, the manual of life, Bhagavad Gita, teaches us how to control anger.

HOW TO USE YOUR EMOTIONS TO GROW

Emotions are the lifeblood of the human experience. They're the driving forces that shape our decisions, actions, and reactions.

Yet, many of us struggle to manage our emotions, especially the uncomfortable ones. Consequently, we end up feeling controlled by them. So, mastering our emotions isn't just a luxury; it's a necessity for enhancing the quality of our lives.

Most people tend to deal with emotions in one of four ways. Some attempt to avoid them, sidestepping their true feelings. Others try to resist or deny their emotions, a method bound to fail since emotions build up until they inevitably erupt. Then, some make emotions a competition, challenging others with sentiments like, "You think *you* feel bad. Well, I feel even worse!"

Constantly suppressing your emotions can lead to insomnia, anxiety, exhaustion, and reduced willpower, which can result in problems with alcohol or overeating.

You can train your brain to build a high level of emotional strength.

So, how do we build emotional strength? Do some people have larger sums in their resilience bank accounts than others? How can we make more deposits than withdrawals? Does it happen naturally over time, or can we train ourselves to be more mentally tough? The overarching answer is simple. Emotional strength is like any muscle.

To truly master your emotions, follow these three steps of emotional mastery called I.M.C. (Table P22.1).

1. Identify the emotion: The first step is *always* to identify the negative emotion – or, more accurately – the *action signal*. What type of emotion is it? Frustration? Sadness? Are you simply hungry? Which emotion are you *really* feeling?
2. Learn the message the emotion is giving you.

TABLE P22.1

Steps of Emotional Mastery

EMOTION I FEEL	THE MESSAGE IS...
Joy	Take some actions
Sadness	Adjust your expectation
Fear	Prepare yourself for the worst
Frustration	Change your perspective
Shame	There is something wrong with me
Loneliness	Build more meaningful connection
Gratitude	I am enough
Guilt	Work on your value system
Discomfort	Change your direction and strategy.

3. Focus on things that you can control

Spend their time and energy focusing on situations and events they control. And because they put their efforts where they can have the most impact, they feel empowered and confident.

Uncovering the core emotion will empower you to discover its value. To truly master our emotions and gain a deep sense of emotional meaning, we must proactively nurture the positive emotions we *want* to feel. Whether it's more love and warmth or more drive and unshakable confidence, the best way to strengthen them is through habitual practice.

When it comes to being a company executive, much more emotional volatility is involved than many realize. You must find ways to ride your emotional highs toward success, double-check yourself during peaks and valleys, and view stress as an opportunity to increase your focus. By channeling your emotions correctly, you will be off the emotional rollercoaster ride and will continue to build momentum for years to come – the sky's the limit.

LEADERSHIP CHALLENGE

Practice the I.M.C. consistently to gain mastery over your emotions.

Part 3

It's Not Lonely at the Top: It's Lonely All the Way to the Top

It's Not Lonely at the Top, It's Lonely All the Way

As I write this chapter, sitting in the living room of my home in Mumbai, India, the window of which opens into the Arabian Sea, enjoying the sea breeze, the doorbell rings, and I see a slightly senior-aged woman standing outside my house. She introduces herself as Meenakshi, my new neighbor.

I am a people person, and I draw energy from people. And so, I never miss an opportunity to interact with people. I invited her in and asked my house to help make herbal tea for us. We chatted for some time, and during our conversation, she told me how she lives alone and feels lonely in life as her husband left her many years ago for another woman. She spoke about her life and how she wished life could end sooner for her because of this loneliness. She used the word lonely around five times in our conversation.

That same morning, I visited a company in Mumbai to speak to Karthik, one of the C.E.O.s of a mid-size company, who told me that though he enjoys his work, he has no one to confide in except me as his coach. With his company numbers going south, he is always on the radar as a public figure. His office environment is intense enough, but then there's the media he has to deal with. And he does all of this alone. Loneliness hinders his job performance.

We spoke for some time about his challenge and the way forward. I told him how one can effectively overcome loneliness.

Both the incidents of this day, one with Meenakshi and one with Karthik, took me back in time to my own life.

Now, there is a skinny line between loneliness and being alone. Feeling lonely can be psychological, and one can feel lonely inside a crowd, too. Alone refers to when a person is on their own or when no one is around or present with them and they feel comfortable. Being alone is just a state; you are not with others and feel ok. Loneliness is an emotion that describes a feeling of sadness and unwantedness attributed to not having a connection with others.

Like Reena, you can be lonely despite having a family, a great job, and everything.

DOI: 10.4324/9781003439134-31

During a recent executive coaching session, my client Reena and I were engaged in a conversation about leadership when she made the following statement:

"Payal, I am passionate about leading my team, but I don't feel anyone 'cares or likes me.'" I had to dig deeper to know where she was coming from and why she felt the way she did. Here's what I learned about her.

Reena is a 35-year-old beautiful woman with a good job, is happily married, and has three children. To outsiders, she seems to have a perfect personal and professional life. A husband who is a simple ear, as well, and has taken care of all her comforts. Professionally, she has achieved great heights. Some would call her lucky.

But deep inside, Reena suffers the kind of loneliness that makes her heart ache. She moved to the UK from India twenty-one years ago, met her husband while working in the UK, married, and had three children. Staying in the UK, she slowly lost all connections with her family and friends in India. She made new friends in the UK, but for most of the time, life was just work and home. Her husband wasn't emotionally into her, though she loved him and made him her world. His love, attention, and affection were more toward the children, balancing work and family, and Reena began to feel ignored and unwanted and begged for his care and attention. Because of her life in the UK, she never had many female friends, worked full-time, and had no hobbies.

Sometimes, while looking outside, seeing a group of women talking or having a good time, she'd be hit by a tidal wave of pain. At times, she would see couples with emotional bonds holding hands and focusing on each other, and she would feel deep down sad. She has no other women to do little things with, like go for a walk or catch up for lunch. She lost many years of her career growth in the UK. Life just swept by for her.

Two years ago, she and her husband returned to India to be closer to family. She realized she had never felt at home in the UK. While in India, her husband was posted in Chennai, South India, a place where Reena again felt alone despite a huge home and also because, culturally, she didn't feel she fit in. For years, she has suffered the agony of loneliness. Just telling this story made her cry. She has no idea how to make new friends her age – everyone else seems well-established. She knows the only solution is to put herself out there, expose her vulnerability, and confront her fear of rejection, but this is easier said than done. So she buried herself in doing more work, became famous in her field, and didn't talk about her lonely life to anyone.

And you can be lonely despite being in a high position in the company like John, a 41-year-old Chief Information Officer, earning over $250K in base salary. His life is all about glamor, traveling globally, and having a private jet. He has a group of male and female friends and a large circle of acquaintances. He also participates regularly in marathons. He has won many accolades and awards for his work. He is a big name in his industry. So, what does he have to complain about?

Well, many of his friends are married and have children. John is single and feels increasingly left behind. He has no one with whom he can enjoy the small pleasures of life, like going to watch a movie, having dinner, or just coming home and talking to someone of his own. Professionally, he has no one he can share his fears with because of his position and role.

Because of this, John suffered a crippling amount of depression and was on antidepressants. His life was work, doctor visits, and medicine. All of this was because he was lonely. If you met with John, you would feel he is happy and going about his work. But from the inside, he is broken and emotionless. And he doesn't talk about this to anyone. His condition has led him to stop engaging in self-care and also made him less likely to reach out and connect. Each day, he battles a profound feeling of emptiness. He is hungry for emotional fulfillment, a good relationship, compassion, peace of mind, joy, and equanimity. The absence of emotional support and meaningful relationships and being isolated despite being a public figure made John's journey lonely.

Loneliness is probably the most obvious of the emotions and the easiest for those not in the seat to push away.

I haven't talked to any successful people who didn't feel extreme loneliness.

Drifting apart and getting slightly lonelier is a natural part of life. But when loneliness consumes you from the inside, which is the case for many successful people, it can get gruesome.

It's a feeling so commonly held by successful people that it's become an idiom: "It's lonely at the top." And so, in the journey to get to the top, you must overcome loneliness and not let it consume you. Because, my friend, one thing is guaranteed: it is going to be a lonely journey all the way to the top.

CLIMBING THE GREASY POLE

As a leadership coach, I'm often asked: What is the hardest part about reaching the top? And my response is overcoming loneliness. The next thing I hear from them is, "Yes, true that it's lonely at the top." I disagree with the context of that statement. Coaching for the last eighteen years, I have witnessed that it's not lonely only at the top; it is lonely all the way to the top.

It's an incredibly lonely journey. Why do I say that it is lonely all the way to the top? Because once you decide to move to the top, you will have to work on yourself, your thinking, and your habits. You will focus more on your work than on friends. You will observe a mismatch between your wavelength and ideas and theirs. People might distance themselves from you because they feel uncomfortable with the changes you're making. Maybe they're used to the old you and don't know how to relate to the new and improved you.

The question is, to reach the top, are you ready for this lonely journey? Are you prepared to leave people who were once a part of your circle?

I know people who never wanted to be a C.E.O. because most C.E.O.s in companies they worked for seemed unhappy and lonely. This is one of the core fears I hear about over and over again.

Success, my friend, is associated with being alone, feeling misunderstood, having no support system, and not finding like-minded individuals to share thoughts and emotions.

Today's leaders are lonelier inside than on the outside. Abraham Lincoln, Princess Diana, Winston Churchill, Michael Jackson, and Elvis Presley are notable figures who have openly expressed their struggles with loneliness.

The loneliness driver I've heard of most from other C.E.O.s is the inability to talk with people about the emotional rollercoaster inherent to the role. So few people have experienced it, and those who have are rarely willing or able to be vulnerable and talk about the difficulties they faced. That lack of vulnerability and connection leads to increased loneliness.

Loneliness impacts your performance and decision-making ability because loneliness triggers the stress response within the body, which causes the body to release stress hormones like cortisol and epinephrine and shift its energy and blood supply toward survival functions like fighting and fleeing a perceived danger. This reaction contributes to disrupted sleep, imbalanced hormones, and an increased tendency toward further isolation. It can lead to poor decision-making, inept problem-solving, frustration, dysfunctional teams, and angry and frustrated employees.

BRAVING THE WILDERNESS

Loneliness is a word I am well associated with and have experienced closely in my personal and professional life. I felt lonely every day – maybe not constantly, but definitely every day for nine-plus years. It's an empty pain you feel running down your soul. I've leaned on no one when the times got tough. It has devastated me, broken me, and made me come out stronger than ever, both personally and professionally. But I did not let it eat me, I did not allow it to keep me down on my knees. I learned how to overcome it and make peace with it while leveraging it to my advantage.

Each day, I dragged myself to work and back home. Come snow and the days got shorter, night got longer and my loneliness only increased. It was in those lonely hours that I discovered myself. No one knew the void inside of me. Life was an open battle, with everyone challenging me. How I longed for a little support, but all I got was a cold shoulder. I am sure we all met loneliness in our journey at some point. And in the end, all I learned was how to be strong alone. And when I learned this valuable lesson, my life changed for the better. It all happened in the evening of 2011 while driving my older daughter to swim lessons; I heard a person on the radio say something that changed my life forever and brought it on track. He said, "How you talk to yourself, about yourself, when by yourself, makes all the difference."

This one phrase changed everything for me and in me. I reflected and discovered that I've had problems with self-talk for so long. I was an award-winning negative self-talker. You wouldn't believe the kinds of opportunities I let myself talk myself out of.

After hearing that statement on the radio, I understood that for me and all other leaders who face and will face loneliness in their journey upward, we must realize that overcoming loneliness is realizing that there is no opponent – you're fighting against yourself.

As leaders, we spend our days surrounded by people, so the last thing we expect is to feel alone, but many do. Why? I believe the feeling of loneliness is not a positional issue but rather one of personality.

You are the only person who you will spend your entire life with. From the day you are born to the day you die, you will have yourself for company no matter what. Always remember that you cannot be lonely if you like the person you are alone with.

You must be self-aware, self-dependent, and a self-healer in your journey to the top. The higher you climb, the more you must rely on yourself. You will fall and fail and will need to get back up quickly on your own.

No doubt you have your team, your people, to support you. But ultimately, you have to know how to be comfortable with yourself and depend most on yourself. My father always taught me to have less expectations from others. He often said that the fewer the expectations, the happier you are. The happier you are within, the lesser the loneliness – the more lonely and depressed you feel, the more the need for company. The more joyful and exuberant you become, the less you need company.

While my younger daughter was interning at a hospital, I met a doctor who said she felt most disconnected when she was swamped as an intern and resident. With one emergency after another, she had no time to take care of herself. And so she kind of covered up her loneliness by smoking cigarettes and alcohol. And then she realized that she was running away from herself and that the best way to be happy is to make somebody else happy. She started yoga and meditation and began making others happy through her work as a doctor. That cured her loneliness.

How we talk to ourselves is fundamental in shaping who we become. It influences how we feel about ourselves, what we can achieve, how the world views us, and how we interact.

What are you saying to yourself daily? What are you telling yourself? What are you making yourself believe?

By the way, the more you manage negative conversations, the fewer you have. I often ask myself: How many more people and companies could I have helped if I had refused to listen to my negative self-talk?

I want you to ask yourself a similar question.

What could you do if you pressed the stop button on your negative chatter and pressed play on your powerful self-talk instead?

But leaders must remember that we are not here to make friends but to build relationships. When we realize our job is to build relationships, create trust, and add value, we'll do everything we can to connect with those we lead and create an atmosphere of coaching and collaboration. When that occurs, you are not lonely; you are fully engaged!

The people I know who've made that switch choose to play bigger than they've ever played before. They don't waste time and energy worrying about what might go wrong; they go out and make their dreams come true.

You have to be willing to walk this journey alone because not everyone is going to fit in every part of your journey.

You will need an unbreakable spirit to rise above the impossible, bounce back, and soar high against all odds to get to the top. No matter who you are or your circumstances, you will have the courage to rise above your own "impossible" and walk your path to greatness.

The question is, are you ready to take that lonely journey and make a quantum leap in your life? Are you ready to make it to the top?

Index

A

A.D.D., 43–44
"Aha" moment, 113
Alexander the Great, 100
Ali, Muhammad, 60
Anxious work attachment, 140–141
Armstrong, Louis, 42
Ashikaga Yoshimasa, 68
Atlanta Business Channel, 64
Attention and approval-seeking disorder (A.A.S.D.), 92
Authentic feedback, 89, 90
Authentic leadership, 89

B

Bannister, Roger, 98
Basketball, 120
"Beast Barracks," 142
Betting on yourself, 63
  'figure it out,' 65–66
  gift of imperfection, 67–69
  life design, 66–67
Bhagavad Gita, 142, 146
The Bible, 142
Branding, 112–114
Brin, Sergey, 51
Burnout, 108, 122
Business decision, 118
Business world, xvi, xvii, 6, 13, 24, 98

C

Career tree, 5
Casas, Pablo, 39
Cavafy, Constantine, 65
Chuang-tzu, 95
Churchill, Winston, 154

Collier, Robert, 80
Commanders, 30–31
Conscious mind, 14, 107, 109
Conventional thinking, 44
Corporate politics, 132–135
Cosell, Howard, 40
Critical mistakes, 144–145
C-Suite, 77, 85, 121

D

Decision-making, 24, 36
  fear in, 121
  information and training in, 118
  loneliness impacts in, 154, 155
  speed, 120
Diana, Princess, 154
Distanced thinking, 45, 49
  adjusting focus, 47–49
  steps, 47
  of successful leaders, 46
Distractions, 41–42
Douglass, Fredrick, 67
Dreams, 24, 79, 80, 100, 121
Dyer, Wayne, xviii

E

Edison, Thomas, 143
Emotional decision, 48
Emotional mastery, 147, 148
Emotional strength, 142, 143
  critical mistakes, 144–145
  emotional control, 145–146
  emotional mastery, 147, 148
  emotional volatility, 148
  state of mind, 144
Energy map, 37
External leadership powers, xxiii, xxiv

F

Failures, 11, 82
Fast leader, 119–122
Feedback
    authentic feedback, 89, 90
    genuine feedback, 89
    help to be better leader, 89
    self-reflection, 90–91
    360-degree feedback, 88
Fischer, Bobby, 58
5-minute programming, 108–110
Focus on your game, 39–40
Foreman, George, 60
Fortune 500 company, 18, 45, 133

G

Gallup report, 110
Gandhi, Mahatma, 74
Genuine feedback, 89
Goals, 4, 85, 87, 105, 144; *see also* Long-
    term goals
Growth, 40, 79, 139

H

Hacks, 52
Hard working, 133
Harry Potter, 35
Harvest, 10
    miracles of, 79
    routine and consistency, 80–82
    seed of sowing, 78, 81
High-potential leaders, 8
Huffington, Arianna, 51
Hybrid work model, 55

I

"The Iconic," 27
Immigrants
    internal gratitude, 51
    mentality, 51
    mindset *vs.* traditional mindset, 53
    quality, 52
    to United States, 50, 53
    work, 53

Imposter syndrome, 9, 94
Industrial Revolution, Europe, 12
Inner intuition, 33
Inner leadership power, xxii, xxiii, xxiv, 24
Inner voice, 111, 126
Insecure leader, 129, 130
Internal leadership power, 45, 46
Intuition, 107, 111
"Ithaka," 65

J

Jackson, Michael, 154
Jackson, Stonewall, 58
Johnson, John, 100
Jordan, Michael, 42, 73, 95
Jugaad, 52, 53

K

Kalam, Abdul APJ, 139
Keller, Helen, 129
Key performance indicators (KPIs), 97
Kintsugi, 67, 68
Knocker-uppers, 12

L

Leaders
    empowerment, 131
    feedback approach, 88
    fundamental duty, 129
    insecure leaders, 129–130
    outstanding leaders, 130
    play big by, 84–86
Leadership
    authentic leadership, 89
    power, xviii, xix, xxi, xxii–xxiv, 20, 23,
        29, 30, 43
    wisdom, 85
Lee, Bruce, 104, 106
Lewis, 21
Life plan, 66–67
Lincoln, Abraham, 130, 154
Loneliness, 151–154
    impacts, 154
    self-talk, 155, 156
Long-term goals, 84, 85

Lord Ram, 4
"Love your job, but don't love your
     company", 139

M

Mandela, Nelson, 74
Mangeshkar, Lata, 73
Margin space, 92–94
Mayan ruins, 27, 28
McClellan, George, 58
Mehta, Atit, 44
Meta-leader, 13, 16, 22
     approach, xviii, xx
     leadership powers, 14
     performance improvement, 21–24
     professional powers, 14
     qualities, 14, 17
     and unleash powers, 18–20
Million-dollar asset, 107
Mind
     methods, to achieve impossible
          execute, 99
          focus, 99
          "Mission Possible," 98–99
          observe self-talk, 99
     reading, 27–30, 33
          Commanders, 30–31
          listen and be in moment, 32
          Partner, 31–32
          Supporter, 31
          Thinker, 31
          understand the triggers, 32
"Mission Possible," 98–99

N

NASA, 7
*The New York Times Crossword Puzzle
     Dictionary* (Pulliam), 15

O

Oh the Places You'll Go (Suess), 23
"One thing," 106
Organa, Leia, 130
Outer leadership powers, xxiii, 24
Outstanding leaders, 130

P

Paralympics, Qatar, 97
Partner, 31–32
Passion, 5, 6, 84, 95
The Payal Nanjiani Leadership Podcast
     (Payal), 27, 127
Peak performers, 123, 124
Performance, 21–24, 35, 36, 71, 89, 97, 139,
     143, 154
Picasso, 106
Pillar of excellence, 72, 73
Pillar of relationships, 72–74
Pillar of uniqueness, 72, 74
Play big, 84, 87
     in career life, 87
     by leaders
          purpose, 84–85
          systems, 85–86
Play bold, 84
Play-it-safe paradox, 64
Positive relational energy, 34
Positive relational energy (P.M.E.), 35–37
Predictable leaders, 56
Presley, Elvis, 154
Professional Aspiration Statement
     (P.A.S.), 3, 5, 6, 52, 53
     career tree, 5
     importance, 7
     of Lord Ram, 4
     steps, 6
Professional power, xxii, xxiii, 14, 19, 23, 24

R

Ramayana, 4
"Refrain and Reframe" strategy, 92–94, 96
"Reinventing You," 114
Roosevelt, Theodore, 73
Rowling, J.K., 35

S

Scalable systems, 86
Schumpeter, Joseph A., 116
Secure work attachment, 139–140
Self-image, 75, 113–115
Self-reflection, 90–91

Self-talk, 99, 155, 156
Shadow coaching, 107, 122
Shakespeare, 106
Shikumi, 24
Shiny objects syndrome (S.O.S.), 41, 102–106
Shula, Don, 115
Silent Revolution? (movie), 87
Sow and harvest, 78, 81
Sow the seeds, 78, 81, 82
Spassky, Boris, 58
Speed, 118–120, 122
Sponsor, 72
    attract a sponsor, 72–74
    identification, 75
    importance, 72
Star Wars IV, 130
State of mind, 144
Subconscious mind, 109, 110
Success, 18, 44
    has no age limit, 99–101
    leadership methodology, 84
    pillar
        of excellence, 72, 73
        of relationships, 72–74
        of uniqueness, 72, 74
Successful entrepreneur, 42
Successful leaders, xxiv, 6, 11–12, 107
    distanced thinking technique, 46
    practice, 103
    super-successful leaders, 63
    weekend practice (*see* Weekend practice)
Success Is Within (Payal), 22
Super-successful leaders, 63
Supporter, 31
Sustaining at top, 8–10
    3.0 version, 9
    corn crop, 10–11
    successful leaders, 11–12
Systems, 85–86

T

Teamwork, 128
Telepathy, 33

Thinker, 31
Thinking patterns, 44
3.0 version, 9
360-degree feedback, 88
Traditional mindset *vs.* immigrant
    mindset, 53
2019 Gallup Survey, 84

U

Uniqueness, 72, 74
United States, 34, 35, 142
    born in, 50
    immigrants, 52, 53
    outstanding leaders, 130
Unpredictable leadership, 56, 57
    habits breaking, 59
    internal standards, 57–59
    step outside comfort zone, 60

V

Vasa (ship), 119, 120

W

Wabi-sabi, 67
Weekend practice, 124
    plan, 125
    practice, 125
    read, 126
    reflect, 125
    strengthen instincts, 125–126
    successful people, 124, 127
Whole absolute brutal truth, 13
"Win The Leadership Game," 22
Work attachment
    anxious attachment, 140–141
    secure attachment,
        139–140

Y

Yoon, Nicola, 64

Printed in the United States
by Baker & Taylor Publisher Services